MACHINE
LANDSCAPES

ARCHITECTURES OF THE
POST-ANTHROPOCENE

ARCH
Janu

Guest-edited by
LIAM YOUNG

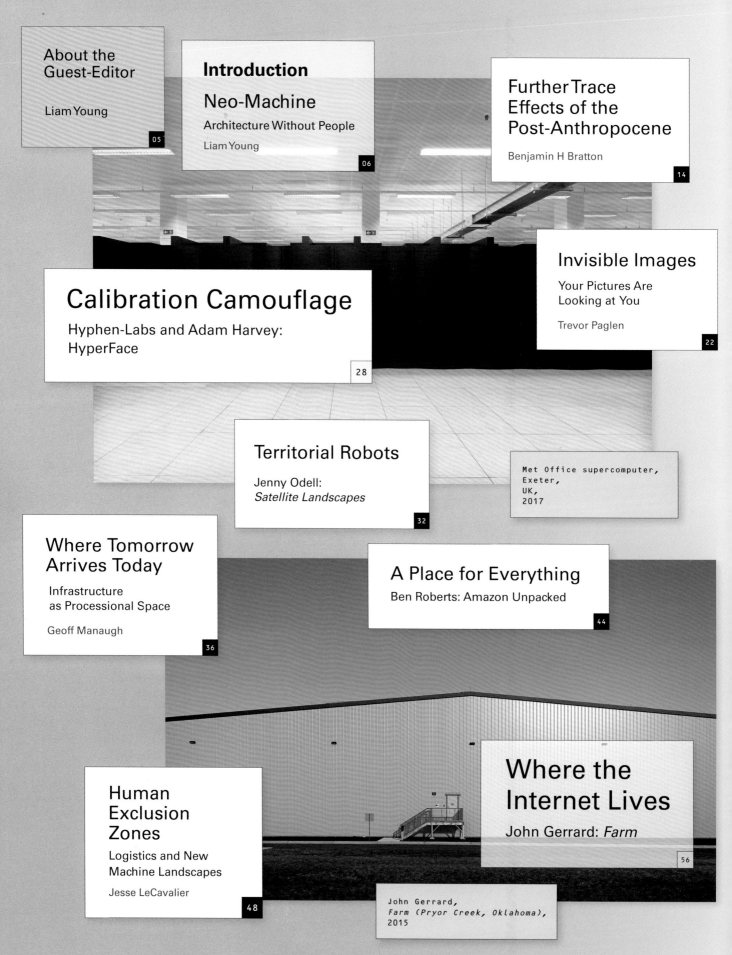

Met Office supercomputer,
Exeter,
UK,
2017

John Gerrard,
Farm (Pryor Creek, Oklahoma),
2015

ISSN 0003-8504
ISBN 978 1119 453017

Boston Dynamics,
SpotMini,
2018

3

Editorial Offices
John Wiley & Sons
9600 Garsington Road
Oxford
OX4 2DQ

T +44 (0)1865 776868

Commissioning Editor
Helen Castle

Managing Editor
Caroline Ellerby
Caroline Ellerby Publishing

Freelance Contributing Editor
Abigail Grater

Publisher
Paul Sayer

Art Direction + Design
CHK Design:
Christian Küsters
and Barbara Nassisi

Production Editor
Elizabeth Gongde

Prepress
Artmedia, London

Printed in Italy by Printer
Trento Srl

Front cover: Ben Roberts,
Amazon Fulfilment
Centre, Rugeley,
Staffordshire, UK, 2011.
© Ben Roberts/Panos

Inside front cover: Jenny
Odell, Manufacturing
Landscape, Benicia Oil
Refinery, California, 2014.
© Jenny Odell

Page 1: Ian Cheng,
*Emissary in the Squat of
Gods* (still), 2015. Image
courtesy of the artist,
Pilar Corrias London,
Gladstone Gallery,
Standard (Oslo)

01/2019

MIX
Paper from
responsible sources
FSC® C015829
www.fsc.org

ARCHITECTURAL DESIGN

January/February
2019

Profile No.
257

Journal Customer Services
For ordering information,
claims and any enquiry
concerning your journal
subscription please go to
www.wileycustomerhelp
.com/ask or contact your
nearest office.

Americas
E: cs-journals@wiley.com
T: +1 781 388 8598 or
+1 800 835 6770 (toll free
in the USA & Canada)

**Europe, Middle East
and Africa**
E: cs-journals@wiley.com
T: +44 (0)1865 778315

Asia Pacific
E: cs-journals@wiley.com
T: +65 6511 8000

Japan (for Japanese-
speaking support)
E: cs-japan@wiley.com
T: +65 6511 8010 or 005 316
50 480 (toll-free)

Visit our Online Customer
Help available in 7 languages
at www.wileycustomerhelp
.com/ask

Print ISSN: 0003-8504
Online ISSN: 1554-2769

Prices are for six issues
and include postage and
handling charges. Individual-
rate subscriptions must be
paid by personal cheque or
credit card. Individual-rate
subscriptions may not be
resold or used as library
copies.

All prices are subject to
change without notice.

Identification Statement
Periodicals Postage paid
at Rahway, NJ 07065.
Air freight and mailing in
the USA by Mercury Media
Processing, 1850 Elizabeth
Avenue, Suite C, Rahway,
NJ 07065, USA.

USA Postmaster
Please send address changes
to *Architectural Design*,
John Wiley & Sons Inc.,
c/o The Sheridan Press,
PO Box 465, Hanover,
PA 17331, USA

Subscribe to ⃝D
⃝D is published bimonthly
and is available to purchase
on both a subscription basis
and as individual volumes
at the following prices.

Prices
Individual copies:
£29.99 / US$45.00
Individual issues on
⃝D App for iPad:
£9.99 / US$13.99
Mailing fees for print
may apply

Annual Subscription Rates
Student: £90 / US$137
print only
Personal: £136 / US$215
print and iPad access
Institutional: £310 / US$580
print or online
Institutional: £388 / US$725
combined print and online
6-issue subscription on
⃝D App for iPad: £44.99 /
US$64.99

Liam Young is a speculative architect and director who operates in the spaces between design, fiction and futures. He is the co-founder of Tomorrow's Thoughts Today, an urban futures think-tank exploring the local and global implications of new technologies, and Unknown Fields, a nomadic research studio that travels on expeditions to chronicle these emerging conditions as they occur on the ground. He has been acclaimed in both mainstream and architectural media, including the BBC, *Wired*, the *Guardian*, Channel 4 and *Vice*, and is producer of a BAFTA-nominated film. His work has been collected by institutions such as the Metropolitan Museum of Art in New York, the Victoria and Albert Museum in London and the Museum of Applied Arts and Sciences in Sydney. He has taught internationally at the Architectural Association (AA) in London and Princeton University in New Jersey, and now runs the groundbreaking MA in Fiction and Entertainment at the Southern California Institute of Architecture (SCI-Arc) in Los Angeles. His narrative approach sits between documentary and fiction, exploring distant landscapes and visualising the future worlds that he extrapolates from them. ◮

ARCHITECTURE
NEO

Met Office supercomputer,
Exeter, UK,
2017

The Cray XC40 is the most powerful supercomputer
on the planet dedicated to weather and climate.

WITHOUT PEOPLE

MACHINE

The most significant architectural spaces in the world are now entirely empty of people. We are going on a tour through these sites, to visit the landscapes and structures made for and by our machines. We begin in a series of anonymous towns in the middle of Oregon where we are visiting the largest cultural landscape in human history. Here, sitting at the confluence of cool air, cheap hydropower and tax incentives the tech giants of Facebook, Google, Apple and Amazon have built their data centres. The chilly breeze that brushes our face has set in motion a storm of infrastructure. This is where the Internet lives.

The Buildings Where We Keep the World

These unremarkable streets and sprawling periphery contain everything about who we are. All of our dreams and fears, histories and futures are here, just behind an Oregon Thriftway, drenched in the stench of diner pancakes and simulation syrup. If we were to stroll through the screen and follow the fibre-optic tentacles across the planet we would find ourselves in unfamiliar places like this, in the autonomous server farms, power plants, ports, factories and mines that produce the modern world.

One of these towns is Prineville, home to Facebook. This is a town that turns electricity into bits, and its data centres are giant machines for organising our culture and archiving our lives. Every like, love letter, embarrassing photo and ironic update is stored in the purring technologies contained in its vast concrete boxes. This intricate portrait of human history is sitting somewhere along a winding two-lane road, near a parking lot, beside a tree, baking in the afternoon sun.

We stroll through the hot aisles, breathing the air that was warmed by our digital selves.

The Facebook Data Center in Prineville, like many similar facilities, is essentially just row upon row of identical floor-to-ceiling server stacks, spinning and writing the lives of 1.9 billion global users. Each of the 4,000 servers in this hall has a blue LED that illuminates when it is accessed, and a yellow flashing light that flickers with the writing of data. The server floor trembles like a forest of fireflies, a map of social-media territory, a spatialised Internet, a field of flickering Facebookers all waving hello. As we exit each room on our tour we diligently switch off the lights. There is no one left behind in the dark; it is a building of empty rooms, quietly humming away without us. Just one Facebook engineer is able to maintain 25,000 servers each day. We are surplus to the practical needs of the data centre. It is a landscape filled with our digital avatars, but strangely absent of people. Just a few wandering techs stalk the aisles, babysitting the servers, watching the lights, waiting for something to do.

The Facebook Data Center is a prime example of one of the new typologies of the posthuman, a building of extraordinary meaning that sits at the core of what it means to exist today, but at the same time turns its back on any expression of that significance. At first glance, there appears to be little architecture here, no grand monumental gesture; instead, this network of spaces so fundamental to our modern experience of the world seems to be conceived of as little more than air-conditioning infrastructure. Architecture has always been defined by the prevailing means of production. Stonemasons once carved column capitals and

Cyrille Dubreuil,
The Bow # 8,
2018

The anonymous and faceless facades of these logistics buildings stand in radical contrast to streets of screaming shopfronts that characterise the shopping malls they are replacing.

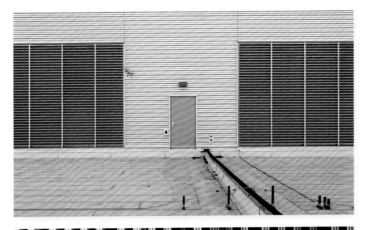

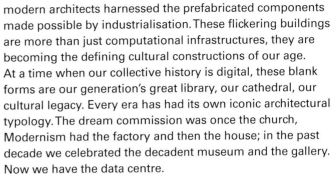

modern architects harnessed the prefabricated components made possible by industrialisation. These flickering buildings are more than just computational infrastructures, they are becoming the defining cultural constructions of our age. At a time when our collective history is digital, these blank forms are our generation's great library, our cathedral, our cultural legacy. Every era has had its own iconic architectural typology. The dream commission was once the church, Modernism had the factory and then the house; in the past decade we celebrated the decadent museum and the gallery. Now we have the data centre.

Sheehan Partners,
Facebook Data Center,
Prineville, Oregon,
2012

left top: The Prineville Data Center is an icon of the technological sublime where incalculable awe is no longer cast across an untamed nature, but intricately bundled cables of turquoise and purple, white noise and the concrete geologies of vast data complexes.

left: A typical server cabinet at Facebook uses 24,000 kilowatt-hours a year, twice the load of two average family homes. Sitting beside the Oregon river hydro-plant, energy is cheap in Prineville, about half the cost of elsewhere in the US, and that is why all the data centres are here.

Met Office supercomputer,
Exeter, UK,
2017

below: The UK's Met Office facility is the most powerful supercomputer on the planet dedicated to weather and climate.

Human Exclusion Zones

In order to understand and chronicle the emerging condition that the data centre embodies, we will push open the pressurised doors and cross the lines of the human exclusion zones to trespass through the machine landscapes that run the world. The server farms, telecommunications networks, distribution warehouses, unmanned ports and industrialised agriculture that define the very nature of who we are today are at the same time places we can never visit. Instead they are occupied by processors and hard drives, logistics bots and mobile shelving units, autonomous cranes and container ships, robot vacuum cleaners and connected toasters, driverless tractors and taxis.

When early explorers were charting the new world, they would load up their ships and head off the map on expansive journeys with uncertain ends. They were pioneers plotting out new lands and foreign territories, strange and unfamiliar although anything but empty. In this issue of *Δ* we map the less-trodden sites, architectures and infrastructures of a system not built for us, but whose form, materiality and purpose is configured to anticipate the logics of machine vision and habitation rather than our own. It is a compendium of conversations and encounters, travels and incursions in landscapes where we do not belong. *Machine Landscapes* is a collection of spaces filled with autonomous natives, where we are each an intruder in an architecture that has left us behind.

We begin the tour with Benjamin Bratton as our guide, sifting through the trace effects of this new age and taking us through a sample set of the constituent conditions of the emerging machine world. With John Gerrard we fly over the tank-proof fence to explore the ventilation towers and manicured lawns of Google's data repository. Ingrid Burrington takes us on a visit to the Amazon wind farms, an energy landscape spinning our Internet into being. In remote mountains we explore the caverns of cryptocurrency miners with photojournalist Xingzhe Liu, and on the coast Geoff Manaugh dodges the robot cranes that load the GPS-controlled container ships with our worldly wares. We follow the trail of rolling machines into the Amazon fulfilment centres where Jesse LeCavalier watches them rumble beneath the pallets from the edges of the human exclusion zones. Clare Lyster surveys a bestiary of bots that form a nomadic infrastructure of everything, Simone Niquille explores the domestic habitat of the SpotMini robot dog, and Tim Maughan careens through the smart city stretched out on the back seat of a driverless car. Deborah Harrison meets the chatbots that live here, and Trevor Paglen captures how different the world looks through their machine-vision eyes. In the skies above, a swarm of unmanned satellites and space junk hurtles through space as archaeologist Alice Gorman pieces together their history and through their orbiting cameras Jenny Odell captures the extent of this vast, autonomous Earth on the edge of change.

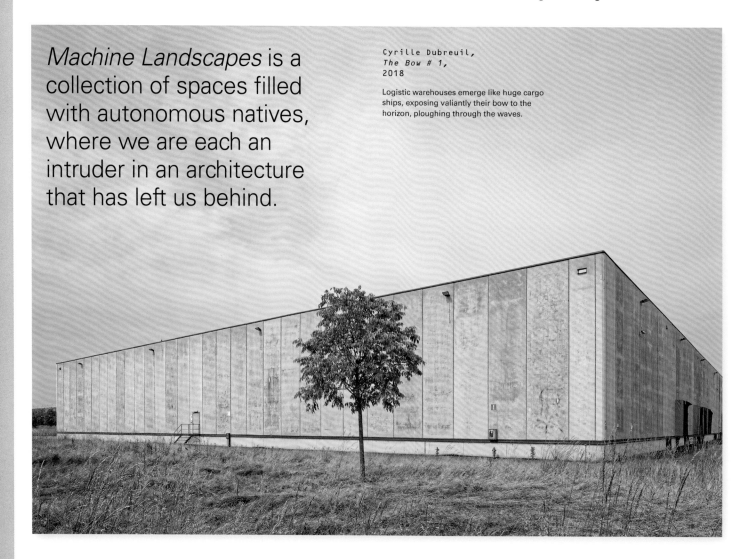

Machine Landscapes is a collection of spaces filled with autonomous natives, where we are each an intruder in an architecture that has left us behind.

Cyrille Dubreuil,
The Bow # 1,
2018

Logistic warehouses emerge like huge cargo ships, exposing valiantly their bow to the horizon, ploughing through the waves.

An Atlas of the Post-Anthropocene

Across the issue, these pioneer landscapes come together to form an atlas, a collection of disconnected territories that constitute an aggregate geography and a portrait of this emerging world. We believe we are living in a new geological epoch, the Anthropocene, where humans are the dominant force shaping the planet, where our own acts of design have forever changed the composition of the atmosphere, the oceans and the Earth. Architecture is a geological force and we have machined the Earth, from the scale of the electron to the tectonic plate.

Ancient craftsmen once measured using parts of the human body: the cubit is based on the length of a forearm; the inch, the length of a thumb. Le Corbusier designed his buildings based around the Modulor, a scale he derived from the proportions of the human body. We once understood our world through systems that positioned ourselves, human scale, vision and patterns of occupation at the centre of the structures that we design. In the age of the network, however, the body is no longer the dominant measure of space; instead it is the machines that occupy the spaces that now define the parameters of the architecture that contains them – an architecture whose form and materiality is configured to anticipate the logics of machine perception and comfort rather than our own.

Spaces that were once bound by the proportions of the body, patterns and cycles of human living, the ambitions of beauty and comfort are now stripped bare and are hazardous zones of toxic air, high-speed robotics, sensor calibration markers, algorithmic complexity and machine scales as inhospitable as the most powerful engine room. We very rarely get our hands dirty, and if we do it is not with any kind of agency, but as optimised bodies engineered as components in this planetary-scaled robot.

The travels through the spaces in this _D_ more accurately map out an era of the Post-Anthropocene as Bratton has defined it,[1] a new age of nonhuman actors where it is technology and artificial intelligence that now compute, condition and construct our world. The issue makes visible an uneven geography where the largest and most critical areas of our cities are now the least occupied. We are constructing an architecture without people. This is not a 'posthuman' condition in the sense this term is typically used. It is not about body modifications, cyborgs, exoskeletons and genetic engineering. The sites that constitute the Post-Anthropocene have nothing to do with our bodies; they are more accurately extra-human in that they are outside us, totally indifferent to us, where we are no longer part of the equation at all.

Cyrille Dubreuil,
The Bow # 6,
2018

The boom of the e-commerce industry has fundamentally transformed the landscape and architecture of the city's periphery. Blank buildings containing a world of objects ready to be boxed up and shipped out are the new face of retail.

Foster + Partners,
Apple Campus,
Cupertino,
California,
2017

The architects' giant doughnut
design houses the headquarters
of Apple, the richest technology
company in the world.

NBBJ,
Amazon Spheres,
Seattle,
Washington,
2017

Architects NBBJ have designed a
breakout space for Amazon workers.
The transparent domes house vertical
gardens and informal relaxation and
meeting rooms to bring employees
'closer to nature'.

The Technological Sublime

We begin to make sense of a new phenomenon by naming it and framing it through mechanisms we find familiar. To assimilate the unknowns of the natural world we first understood it through mythology and folklore. Gods pulled the sun across the sky and sea monsters crashed waves across ships. Then our objective scientific eye categorised nature, developing classes and species, and all fell into line. Machine landscapes are typologies without history. They are sites that force us to question all we know of architecture, and we must again re-evaluate our own position in relation to the spaces and systems around us. So many of these evidentiary artefacts of this emerging era suggest new typologies or call out the inefficiencies of architectural conventions based around our own bodies that until now have seemed satisfactory. We do not have sufficient terminology to describe these conditions; they emerged in the shadows, out of sight, in territories where we are not allowed to wander. They occur at scales where the disciplinary language of architecture breaks down, where interiors become so vast that they become microclimates, where landscapes are so engineered they become circuit boards, where robots become so ubiquitous they become nature, where aisles through the server stacks are like partitions on a hard drive and buildings are so full of machines that they are better understood as urban-scale computers. The core ambitions upon which the architectural profession is founded are being brought into question by these machine structures. These projects are rarely discussed in the design press, but are so fundamental to the cities we all live in. This issue of ⌀ is an early map, an atlas fraught with gaps and contradictions, but an initial attempt to chronicle these conditions as they occur on the ground so that we may develop new relationships to a context evolving faster than our culture can keep up with.

The marquee architectures of technology are the corporate headquarters of BIG and Heatherwick Studio's Googleplex, Foster + Partners' Apple Campus and NBBJ's Amazon Spheres. These are not the star architects of the Post-Anthropocene. They are just set-dressing the waiting rooms …

Once the definition of a new territory has been outlined we need to come to some consensus of what to do next. Do we go to war, do we colonise or sneak our way in, or do we stand at the edges and watch on from afar? The world without us is not the result of some apocalyptic event that wiped us out, but a gradual development, the origins of which can be traced back to the Industrial Revolution. The architects of server farms and data centres, logistics warehouses, the streets of the driverless car, production lines and factory floors have been operating behind the scenes for some time, silently constructing everything and everywhere. Falling into the Post-Anthropocene does not mean the abandoning of all that came before it. It necessitates an understanding that our technology is, as geology, a system that has resonate effects through deep history and even deeper futures. These sites are not warning signs, they are not cautionary tales of what could happen. This is not about the fear of redundancies through automation or the threat of machines out of control, but an emerging landscape of opportunities generated precisely because we can stay away.

Ideology rarely evolves at the pace of our technology. As we turn our gaze towards the machine landscapes, we need to radically embrace our uncomfortable place in a world where we are no longer at its centre. These extra-human sites are the precursors of a new aesthetic and formal movement, a technological sublime. This issue marks an end to human-centred design as we now chart an era of hard-drive-centred design, LIDAR-centred design or autonomous-car-centred design.

The default position of the architecture profession seems to be to try to reclaim this lost territory, to sneak back in and parasitically occupy these landscapes with ergonomic furniture, open-plan offices, green walls and raw-juice bars. The marquee architectures of technology are the corporate headquarters of BIG and Heatherwick Studio's Googleplex, Foster + Partners' Apple Campus and NBBJ's Amazon Spheres. These are not the star architects of the Post-Anthropocene. They are just set-dressing the waiting rooms, distracting us with expressive displays while the machines program our planet, hidden behind windowless walls and anonymous forms. While machines burn down the house we are still worried about the shape of its roof. In these new landscapes the poetics of human occupation are extraneous, the scale of the body is immaterial, and we must explore new forms of productive engagement with the nonhuman world. As this atlas attests, the founding machine landscapes of the Post-Anthropocene are already here, critical and fundamental, embedded in the ground of the Earth and the fabric of the planetary city. Their cooling fans spin, the electromagnetics hum, the LEDs flicker and it smells of rare earth. Machines are making the world and we are on the outside peering in, faces pressed to the glass windows of an empty control room. ⌀

Note
1. Benjamin H Bratton, 'Some Trace Effects of the Post-Anthropocene: On Accelerationist Geopolitical Aesthetics', *E-Flux Journal*, 46, June 2013, pp 1–12.

ФОРМАЛЬДЕГИД
содержится в обивке мебели, древесно-стружечных панелях, пенопластовых теплоизоляторах. Может вызвать воспаление глаз, кожи, дыхательных путей, тошноту и головокружение.

АЭРОЗОЛИ
часто содержат 1,1,1-трихлорэтан, парадихлорбензол вызывающие головокружения, перебои дыхания, рак.

ОБЫЧНЫЕ ЗАГРЯЗНИТЕЛИ ПИТЬЕВОЙ ВОДЫ:
мышьяк, кадмий, хром, свинец, ртуть, нитраты, бензол, углеродистый тетрахлорид, хлороформ, диоксины особенно TCDD) дибромид этилена, полихлорированные дифенилы, трихлорэтилен и винилхлорид
МОГУТ ПРИВЕСТИ
К НЕРВНЫМ РАССТРОЙСТВАМ, РАКУ И ДРУГИМ ЗАБОЛЕВАНИЯМ.

FURTHER TRACE
THE POST-ANTH

No geological age lasts forever. After the Anthropocene, in which human activity became the dominant influence on the planet, the Post-Anthropocene is dawning. What does this entail? California-based architectural and design theorist **Benjamin H Bratton**, who holds professorships and leads teaching programmes in the US, Switzerland and Russia, offers a list of this new era's trace effects that are each both revelatory and catastrophic, from self-composing landscapes to conversing machines and from human exclusion zones to the apparatus of geocinema.

Homo sapiens adult (model) displayed in typical habitat,
State Darwin Museum,
Moscow,
2017

Anthropos of Anthropogeny and anthropos of Anthropocene walk into a bar …

EFFECTS OF
ROPOCENE

If the Anthropocene proves more a fleeting geopolitical instant than a slow geological era – waves of apes maniacally excavating ancient carbon and drawing loops on maps – then whatever comes 'next' would be formed not by the same *anthropos* but by something literally post-, un-, in-'human', for better or worse.[1] So too the cities.

If Anthropogeny is the study of how a species becomes human, then *anthropolysis* may define the process by which it becomes something else.[2] Both are defined by genomic thresholds, but also by how such creatures define themselves, including, for example, the violent tendency to define the human not through the polyphony of all, but in relation to those who count as model and modal ones (animated in no small part by a deeply ingrained capacity – a need, even – to imbue binding narratives with ontological importance).[3]

We might instead see the 'human' as a mutable and untimely figure, not only capable of metamorphoses but inevitably caught within them.[4] The anthropolytic turn, so to speak, would be simultaneously a (small p) promethean demystification and a copernican trauma: culinary interventions into irregular landscapes by hominids demoted from the thrones of legacy illusions. Among these is the conceit that defines 'intelligence' essentially by our experience of our own sapience rather than as an emergent capacity of any matter ordered just so (including what is called AI).

As we learn to measure that in which we have always been embedded but could not perceive until now, we mark both things that have a name but which have not fully arrived and things that have arrived but which are misarticulated or not even named as such. These are the trace effects you are looking for.

Here we count functional intelligence imbued with performances of sensing and effecting, observing and modelling, governing and expressing, etc. They reflect the all-too-human biases of their creators but may also exceed their language altogether, rendering a world that is right at hand but uncannily alien.

The sample subset of these trace effects identified below may prove to be less early signals of what is appearing than maximal signals of what is already present. Even so, the reductive muddle of optimism versus pessimism, utopia versus dystopia is to be avoided. Any of these trace effects is revelatory in some ways and catastrophic in others. It is never only one or the other, but often it is both.

Landscapes Thinking About Landscapes
Through the mineral-based technologies we call 'artificial intelligence', landscapes think about themselves and compose themselves. They may do so in detailed accordance with ideal models and/or as emergent assemblages, stable or fragile: *telos* unless not. This double potential for synthetic ecologies to operate as the shadows of governing simulations, and/or to undermine and eventually collapse that governance by their own weedy means, is a permanent feature.

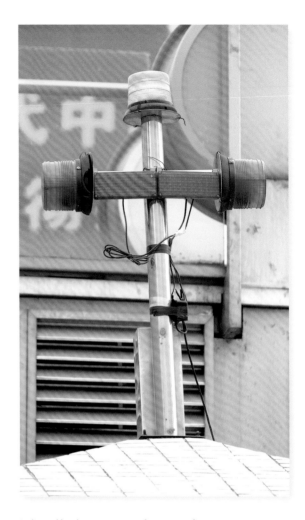

Urban display system of uncertain provenance and purpose, Shenzhen/Hong Kong border, 2018

Signals do not only signal what they signify but also what the signal does.

Seg Electronics Market display in formation, Huaqiang North Road Commercial District, Shenzhen, China, 2018

The stagecraft of landfills is a design genre with many schools of thought.

Boxes Talking to Boxes That Talk to Humans Who Talk to Boxes

All this chattering may be silent or deafening (being another kind of silence). It speaks in blippy tones or with alarmingly natural human voices. Such conversational user interfaces, especially in the form of personified bots, can be used to actively programme complex systems and, as procedural programming shifts toward machine-learning models, may replace command-line and visual programming interfaces. This would have the double effect of collapsing distinctions between using a system and programming it, broadening access to commandability, but also obfuscating the layers of the stack at hand which appear as a literal talking black box / metal tube.

IONLPT (Internet Of Natural Language Processing Things)

With the ubiquity of inexpensive machine learning chips spread into the fabric of the world, language-as-interface may encompass more of machine-to-machine communication as well. The high end of Moore's Law, where natural language processing (NLP) is honed, feeds the lower end, seeding the little cheap chips with the ability to speak and understand English or 中文. The car may tell the garage to open by literally saying 'Garage: I am the Car, open up!' The IONLPT (Internet Of Natural Language Processing Things) suggests a sensing landscape in which signals become semantics and those semantics become an active overlay onto physical space. Here identity-layer authentication systems crisscross boundaries of single, plural and composite users: animal, vegetable and/or mineral.

An Agriculture of Statistics

Such chatter may be mediated by large cloud platforms, but it need not be exclusively so. Still the federation of multiple threads of conversation into the derivative macromodels from which patterns can be seen and acted upon by anyone or everyone requires its own special cities. Such server 'farms' are where this agriculture of statistics is cultivated by kilometre-by-kilometre cloud landscapes growing in pace with widening bandwidth channels. At continental scale, the geopolitical subdivision into multipolar hemispherical stacks – GAFA (Google, Apple, Facebook, Amazon), BAT (Baidu, Alibaba, Tencent) etc – intensifies programmes of governance through models drawn from sovereign data caches. The models live in this post-boring sprawl of fortified energy sinks: shadow cities full of partial, disposable avatars of you, me and the climate we ride on.

Machine Husbandry: Risk vs Riskiness

Down the road, automation at manufacturing and logistics scale includes not just machines talking to each other but making one another as well. If Tinder is how AI breeds humans, then automated manufacturing is how it breeds machines. As the automation of key economic interfaces such as shipping ports intensifies and diversifies, it focuses political attention upon them. Automation brings risks that are both certain and uncertain but the societal comprehension of these can be obtuse. The net benefit of automated vehicles (AV), including driverless cars, may save hundreds of thousands of lives a year, but in the meantime, every accident in which they are involved is shown as proof of a conspiracy of negligence.

AshCloud factory,
Shenzhen,
China,
2018

Automation as ambiance: boxes in the far end of the garden of robots where phone cases are harvested. Design style for future live/work/cafe.

Homo sapiens child wearing festive duck mask,
La Jolla,
California,
2017

The industrial pastoral gets more recent as years pass, but camouflage persists.

The perceived risk of strange things is usually greater than the presumed risk of the status quo, even if that is regular carnage. Moreover, design's most decisive impacts are usually indirect; they are more like trophic cascades within an ecological chain than simple cause meets effect. For example, the modelling of risk by insurance companies is the slow hand of automotive design, making the rolling machines lighter, more energy efficient and crash resistant because the industry's predictive models of the future govern their present (indeed *how* we model the past frames how we model the future, which decides the boundaries of the present).

Trophic Cascades and the Parable of Pig Organ Cities

Yet – as Lucien, my 10-year-old son, reminds me – if we save all those people in car crashes, where will organs for transplantation come from? Road deaths are the primary source of transplanted organs, and so shall we turn to growing new organs, perhaps in genetically modified pigs? As it turns out, outfitting cars with advanced sensors and effectors may have the cascading effect of fast-tracking the deregulation of CRISPR gene-editing technology and zoning for pig farms. In the near term, the design of AV will likely also be governed by liability mandates, which would in turn affect how AV redesigns the cities around them. While the surface area of cities may be opened up by the disappearance of parking lots no longer needed to store individual user vehicles in a suspended state, the definition of 'streets' may change as AVs and the ambulatory humans formerly known as 'pedestrians' are kept at a secure distance from each other. In such a world, human zones may be more park-like, but robots take the streets.

Learning to Live With (But Not In) Human Exclusion Zones

Today automation's most comfortable environment is within the bubble of the factory, where humans are kept safe from potentially dangerous robots and where robotics grows sheltered from both vandalism and conventional expectations of how occupied areas should be programmed. Automation at urban scale may mean opening the factory doors and generalising its environmental motifs more widely. Bringing automated factory logics into the city means learning to live with (if not in) human exclusion zones. These include the aforementioned AV corridors; but, even as some 'factory' protocols seep into everyday life human–robotics interaction and intermixing, at regional scale the boundaries may be hardened. That is, the differentiation between the urban core as a front-stage zone for human residence and entertainment versus 'rural' peripheral back-stage zones for automated agriculture, manufacturing, logistics and energy harvesting is drawn more distinctly.

Automation Becomes Ambiance

While membranes between human zones and human exclusion zones are fortified, this is not the same as a clear delineation between city and 'countryside' as territorial typologies. It is all 'city' in different shades and stripes and relative densities. At the sprawling edge where food and energy come from, backstage urban megainteriors can look more like geoengineering in a petri dish than architecture. We do not have a nuanced language to describe them on their

Factory automation programming in the urban wild,
Heathrow Terminal 5,
London,
2018

Human exclusion zones and human inclusion zones
render the city with the automation ambiance.

TODAY AUTOMATION'S
MOST COMFORTABLE
ENVIRONMENT IS
WITHIN THE BUBBLE OF
THE FACTORY, WHERE
HUMANS ARE KEPT SAFE
FROM POTENTIALLY
DANGEROUS ROBOTS

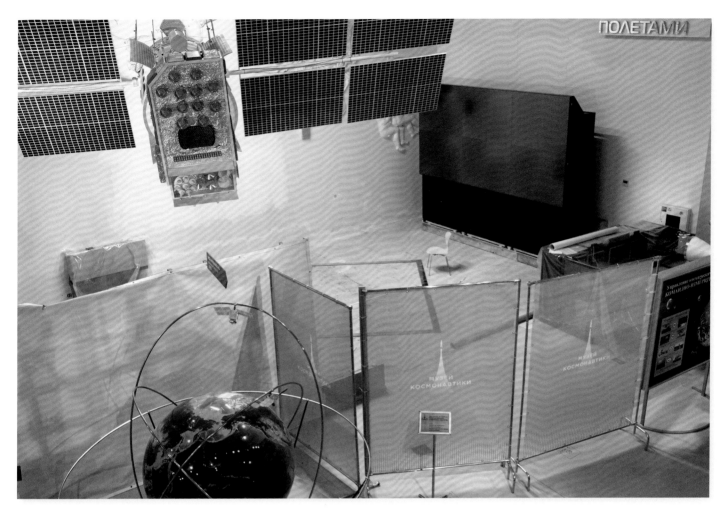

own terms because, even as so-called 'industrial architecture' may be where many of the most interesting technological and intellectual disciplinary problems are now situated, it has little prestige. Theoretically rich coffee-table books of best-in-class automated power plants, warehouses, megafarms etc are required.

In the meantime, the mingling of some people with everyday urban robotics will also mean the displacement of others, in retail spaces for example. Cashierless retail dispenses with some older forms of customer experience theatre but introduces others, stripping the supply chain down to a single interface or arranging touch-and-feel showrooms. Service design becomes the stagecraft by which automation becomes ambiance with its own aesthetic range.

Planetary Protection and its Agencies

The extreme of human exclusion zones is recommended by setting half the Earth's surface aside for recovery, rewilding, remediation, repair and return to other evolutionary selection pressures.[5] The subsequent concentration of the human terrestrial domain into denser urban apparatuses, inclusive of their own narrowly defined smaller exclusion zones, would contain us in a synthetic garden surrounded immediately by automated landscapes, and at further distance by other ecologies with trajectories of their own. This should be seen not as some metaphysical cleavage of culture from nature but rather enforced division as a technology of heterogeneity.[6] It is perhaps an application to Earth of some best practices that NASA's Office of Planetary Protection developed for Mars.[7]

Memorial Museum of Cosmonautics, Moscow, 2017

From globalisation to planetarity: the space race became the time race, which became an archive of satellites.

Geocinema, Simulation and How They See Us Seeing Through Them

For such re-sortings, humans are simultaneously contained within our habitats and now living with and among robotics so thoroughly that we never bother to actually call them 'robots'. Their administrative constitutions are written as/by model simulations of the specific worlds they are capable of sensing and conceiving. 'The visible is in the eye of the beholder' (as Sandy Alexandre said at MIT's 'Being Material' symposium in April 2017),[8] and so the socio-perceptive function of machine vision may be quite different in different zones of the expanded city. Landscapes capable of processing light into information – sensation into semantics – find different purposes to describe, predict and prescribe what they see on behalf of different models. In any complex ecology there are incentives to hide, to scan, to camouflage, to self-display and to trick the world into seeing things not as they are but as they could be or should be. Yet, while machine vision may be crucial input for the model simulations through which landscapes govern themselves, the status of 'representation' in how deep learning systems are trained is itself undecided.

At planetary scale, we see the formation of a vast geocinematic apparatus built from roving satellites, surveillance cameras, geosensing arrays, billions of cellphones etc, producing not one master image but multiple possible composites each of which overflows frames of perception. We have yet to really discover what kinds of cinema we can compose with this already existing apparatus – what durations, what perspectives, what contortions of narrative, what distribution of 'screens' – but the answers will define visual culture: an archive of/for an uncertain future-present. The whole of the source material is too large and comes too fast to see at once, and so secondary summary images are calculated into interactive diagrams that help carve the staggering noise of all-images-at-once into graspable form.

The social scope of data at this scale is not just panoptic policing, but also the deep recursion between natural simulation and design. As its projective models of the future seep into the present, simulation itself becomes the hand of design, because for the simulation the past, the present and the future are just different states within the same model. Can they, thereby, slow our governing models to the pace of the ecological patterns that require our most earnest attention and creative engagement?

Sorrento Valley, California, 2018

The good Post-Anthropocene. The angel of collapse cult is sunset emoji.

HUMAN INTELLIGENCE IS A FUNCTION OF ITS SITUATED EMERGENCE WITHIN A SPECIFIC, BIOCHEMICAL PLANETARY CONDITION FROM WHICH IT CANNOT ESCAPE WITHOUT BECOMING SOMETHING ELSE.

Disclosures

These are only a few relevant trace effects drawn from and for the thematics of this issue of Δ. Others, equally essential, have little to do with what we recognise as 'technological', but in different combinations they point towards other cosmotechnics – a term borrowed from Yuk Hui that refers to the slippage and bindings between a historically embedded social ontology and a society-scale technical system. The same tools may be comprehended as utterly different things which bring quite different disclosures. That is, new technologies not only provide for new affordances, and evolve in relation to the intermingling of functions and counter-functions, but can also, in their emergence, reveal things that have been there all along, but which were difficult or impossible to perceive without them. Can we foresee a cosmotechnics that engages these trace effects as disclosing paths to vibrancy, survival, heterogeneity and demystification – and, if so, at what cost?

Such a perspective must resist the tendency to reduce the complexity of the system itself to the complexity of the control system we use to think, compose and govern it. For that, the design project must hold that deep time runs in both directions, not only into the geological past but also into given and un-given futures, and back around and through. If the dominant steerage remains, carrying on as if the reified subjective experience is more real than real, then the Post-Anthropocene 'we' make may be more Plutocene, a biochemical catastrophe that tears at all life. Human intelligence is a function of its situated emergence within a specific, biochemical planetary condition from which it cannot escape without becoming something else. That becoming may happen anyway, with or without escape, but for it to find a way it demands a re-dedication to the open wound of our geological perch. Δ

Notes

1. See Benjamin H. Bratton, 'Some Trace Effects of the Post-Anthropocene: On Accelerationist Geopolitical Aesthetics', *E-flux Journal* 46, June 2013: www.e-flux.com/journal/46/60076/some-trace-effects-of-the-post-anthropocene-on-accelerationist-geopolitical-aesthetics/.
2. See Benjamin H Bratton, 'On Anthropolysis', in Nick Axel, Beatriz Colomina, Nikolaus Hirsch, Anton Vidokle, Mark Wigley (eds), *Superhumanity: The Design of the Self*, University of Minnesota Press (Minneapolis), 2018, pp 373–8.
3. See Robert N Bellah, *Religion in Human Evolution: From the Paleolithic to the Axial Age*, Harvard University Press (Cambridge, MA), 2011.
4. See Reza Negarestani, 'The Labor of the Inhuman', in Armen Avanessian and Robin Mackay (eds), *#Accelerate: The Accelerationist Reader*, Urbanomic (Falmouth and Berlin), 2014, pp 425–66.
5. See Kim Stanley Robinson, 'Empty Half the Earth of its Humans: It's the Only Way to Save the Planet', 20 March 2018: www.theguardian.com/cities/2018/mar/20/save-the-planet-half-earth-kim-stanley-robinson.
6. Bernard Stiegler, *Neganthropocene*, edited and translated by Daniel Ross, Open Humanities Press (London), 2017.
7. https://planetaryprotection.nasa.gov/about.
8. Quoted in Julia Buntaine, 'Roundup: "Being Material" at MIT's Center for Art, Science & Technology', *Sciart Magazine*, 27 April 2017: www.sciartmagazine.com/blog/roundup-being-material-at-mits-center-for-science-art-technology.

Trevor Paglen

Invisible Images

Your Pictures Are Looking at You

What are the implications of computer vision in relation to machine learning and 'artificial intelligence'? New York-based artist and writer **Trevor Paglen** argues that autonomous image-interpretation systems, from algorithms that analyse photos on Facebook to licence-plate readers used by police, constitute a new kind of visuality which is paradoxically largely invisible to human eyes. What is more, this new 'invisible visuality' should be understood as a means of centralising power in the hands of the state and corporate actors who are able to deploy machine-vision systems at scale.

Trevor Paglen,
Shadow (Corpus: Things that Exist Negatively),
'Adversarially Evolved Hallucination' series,
2017

Paglen's 'Invisible Images' body of work, to which all six of the dye sublimation prints shown in this article belong, has been formed over years of his collaboration with software developers and computer scientists.

Our eyes are fleshy things, and for most of human history our visual culture has also been made of fleshy things. The history of images is a history of pigments and dyes, oils, acrylics, silver nitrate and gelatin – materials that one could use to paint a cave, a church or a canvas. One could use them to make a photograph, or to print pictures on the pages of a magazine. The advent of screen-based media in the latter half of the 20th century was not so different: cathode ray tubes and liquid crystal displays emitted light at frequencies our eyes perceive as colour, and densities we perceive as shape.

We have got pretty good at understanding the vagaries of human vision; the serpentine ways in which images infiltrate and influence culture, their tenuous relationships to everyday life and truth, the means by which they are harnessed to serve – and resist – power. The theoretical concepts we use to analyse classical visual culture are robust: representation, meaning, spectacle, semiosis, mimesis and all the rest. For centuries these concepts have helped us to navigate the workings of classical visual culture.

But over the last decade or so, something dramatic has happened. Visual culture has changed form. It has become detached from human eyes and has largely become invisible. The overwhelming majority of images are now made by machines for other machines, with humans rarely in the loop. The advent of machine-to-machine seeing has been barely noticed, and poorly understood by those of us who have noticed, even as the landscape of invisible images and machine vision becomes ever more active. Its continued expansion is starting to have profound effects on human life. Invisible images are actively watching us, poking and prodding, guiding our movements, inflicting pain and inducing pleasure. This relationship between human viewers and images is a critical function to analyse – but it is exactly this assumption of a human subject that I want to question.

What is truly revolutionary about the advent of digital images is the fact that they are fundamentally machine-readable: they can only be seen by humans in special circumstances and for short periods of time. A photograph shot on a phone creates a machine-readable file that does not reflect light in such a way as to be perceptible to a human eye. A secondary application, like a software-based photo viewer paired with a liquid crystal display and backlight, may create something that a human can look at, but the image only appears to human eyes temporarily. However, the image does not need to be turned into human-readable form in order for a machine to do something with it. This is fundamentally different from a film negative, which is unreadable by humans and machines alike.

The fact that digital images are fundamentally machine-readable regardless of a human subject has enormous implications. It allows for the widespread automation of vision, as well as the exercise of power on dramatically larger and smaller scales than previously possible.

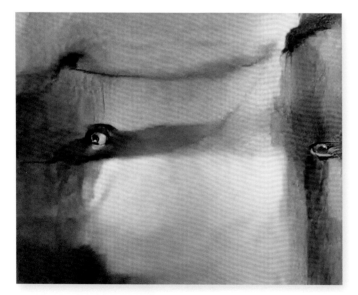

Trevor Paglen,
Human Eyes (Corpus: The Humans),
'Adversarially Evolved Hallucination' series,
2017

AIs operate based on a nominated training set. As a machine is taught to recognise certain features, it inevitably evolves to ignore others. These hidden biases are not politically neutral.

Visual culture has changed form. It has become detached from human eyes and has largely become invisible.

Trevor Paglen,
Babel (Corpus: Spheres of Purgatory),
'Adversarially Evolved Hallucination' series,
2017

Unlike human perception, an AI can never break the rules that are coded into it, meaning its internal politics of meaning and taxonomies are strictly fixed.

Trevor Paglen, *Highway of Death (Corpus: The Aftermath of the First Smart War)*, 'Adversarially Evolved Hallucination' series, 2017

To make the prints in his 'Adversarially Evolved Hallucination' series, Paglen trained an AI to recognise images associated with taxonomies such as omens and portents, monsters and dreams.

Trevor Paglen, *Venus Flytrap (Corpus: American Predators)*, 'Adversarially Evolved Hallucination' series, 2017

To create this image series, AIs were trained on thousands of images that were labelled and tagged in order to teach the AI what it was looking at.

Shifting Visual Culture

Our built environments are filled with examples of machine-to-machine seeing apparatuses: automatic licence-plate readers (ALPRs) mounted on police cars, buildings, infrastructure and private vehicles snap photos of every car entering their frames. ALPR operators, like the company Vigilant Solutions, collect the locations of every car their cameras see, use optical character recognition (OCR) to store licence-plate numbers, and create databases used by police departments or insurance companies. In the consumer sphere, outfits like Euclid Analytics and Realeyes install cameras in malls and department stores to track the motion of people through space with software that identifies who is looking at what for how long, and to track facial expressions of mood and emotional state of shoppers. These systems are only possible because digital images are machine-readable and do not require a human in the analytic loop.

This invisible visual culture is not just confined to industrial operations, law enforcement and 'smart' cities, but extends into what we naively think of as human-to-human visual culture. I am referring here to the trillions of images that humans share on digital platforms – ones that seem to be made by humans for other humans.

On its surface, a platform like Facebook seems analogous to the musty glue-bound photo albums of postwar America. But this analogy is deeply misleading, because something completely different happens when you share a picture on Facebook. When you post, you are feeding an array of immensely powerful artificial-intelligence systems information on how to identify people and how to recognise

places, objects, habits, preferences, race, class, gender identifications, economic statuses and more.

Regardless of whether a human subject actually sees any of the 2 billion photographs uploaded daily to Facebook-controlled platforms, the photographs on social media are scrutinised by neural networks with a degree of attention that would make even the most steadfast art historian blush. Facebook's DeepFace algorithm, developed in 2014 and deployed in 2015, produces facial models and uses a neural network that achieves over 97 per cent identification accuracy. These AI systems have appropriated human visual culture and transformed it into a massive, flexible training set. The more images Facebook and Google's AI systems ingest, the more accurate they become, and the more influence they have on everyday life.

The Role of Abstractions

If we take a peek into the internal workings of machine-vision systems, we find a menagerie of abstractions that seem completely alien to human perception. The machine-to-machine landscape is not one of representations so much as activations and operations. But this is not to say that there is no formal underpinning to how computer-vision systems work.

All computer-vision systems produce mathematical abstractions from the images they are analysing, and the qualities of those abstractions are guided by the kind of metadata the algorithm is trying to read. Facial recognition, for instance, typically involves any number of techniques, depending on the application, the desired efficiency and

We no longer look at images – images look at us. They no longer simply represent things, but actively intervene in everyday life.

Trevor Paglen, *A Man (Corpus: The Humans)*, 'Adversarially Evolved Hallucination' series, 2017

Paglen's *A Man* image shows us the inner machinations of what a neural network thinks a man looks like.

the available training sets. Convolutional neural networks (CNN) are built out of dozens or even hundreds of internal software layers that can pass information back and forth. The earliest layers of the software pick apart a given image into component shapes, gradients, luminosities and corners. Those individual components are convolved into synthetic shapes. Deeper in the CNN, the synthetic images are compared to other images the network has been trained to recognise, activating software 'neurons' when the network finds similarities.

We might think of these synthetic activations as being analogous to a collective unconscious of artificial intelligence – a tempting, although misleading, metaphor. Neural networks cannot invent their own classes; they are only able to relate images they ingest to images that they have been trained on. And their training sets reveal the historical, geographical, racial and socio-economic positions of their trainers. Feed an image of Édouard Manet's painting *Olympia* (1863) to a CNN trained on the industry-standard 'Imagenet' training set, and the CNN is quite sure that it is looking at a burrito, the 'burrito' object class being specific to a young developer diet in the San Francisco Bay Area. On a more serious level, engineers at Google deactivated the 'gorilla' class after it became clear that its algorithms trained on predominantly white faces and tended to classify African Americans as apes.

Relearning How to See
The point here is that if we want to understand the invisible world of machine-to-machine visual culture, we need to unlearn how to see like humans. We need to learn how to see

a parallel universe composed of activations, keypoints, eigenfaces, feature transforms, classifiers and training sets. But it is not just as simple as learning a different vocabulary. Formal concepts contain epistemological assumptions, which in turn have ethical consequences. The theoretical concepts we use to analyse human visual culture are profoundly misleading when applied to the machinic landscape.

To mediate against the optimisations and predations of a machinic landscape, one must create deliberate inefficiencies and spheres of life removed from market and political predations – 'safe houses' in the invisible digital sphere. It is in inefficiency, experimentation, self-expression and often law-breaking that freedom and political self-representation can be found.

We no longer look at images – images look at us. They no longer simply represent things, but actively intervene in everyday life. We must begin to understand these changes if we are to challenge the exceptional forms of power flowing through the invisible visual culture that we find ourselves enmeshed within. ɒ

This is an edited excerpt from a text originally published in *The New Inquiry* on 8 December 2016.

Calibration Camouflage

Hyphen-Labs and Adam Harvey: HyperFace

Facial recognition software raises issues of privacy and perception. To tackle these, **Adam Harvey**, an American designer based in Berlin, has worked with the multinational multimedia collective **Hyphen-Labs** to create a new form of camouflage textile aimed at computer rather than human vision. Guest-Editor Liam Young investigates.

Hyphen-Labs and Adam Harvey,
HyperFace scarf prototype,
2017

opposite: What appears to the human eye as random pixels of black and white is actually, to a facial-recognition algorithm, an ideal representation of a face. This pattern is how machines see a crowd of people.

above: Visualisation of the face-detection activations computed from the patterns of HyperFace images.

The technologies of camouflage have always evolved with the technologies of seeing. The way we look at the world defines how we disappear into it. In the First World War, the fractured geometries painted on dazzle ships deceived the human eye looking down the lens of a periscope, making it difficult to determine a target's range, speed or heading. The inflatable tanks and planes of the Second World War's Ghost Army fooled the analysts hunched over aerial photographs with a magnifying glass. Soldiers uniformed in the disruptive pattern material of the 1960s and 1970s were swallowed by the jungle when seen through the optics of binoculars and sniper scopes. New material technologies of stealth responded to the extended spectrum of vision made possible by radar to render bombing runs invisible to the anti-aircraft guns below. Now the dominant apparatus looking at the world is not the human eye, but machine-vision algorithms and neural nets.

Such technologies see the world through coded sets of rules. Whether through a camera lens, sensor or scanner they search for particular configurations of data, sets of predefined relationships, patterns and geometries. Machine vision abstracts the nuances and complexity of our world so that it can be efficiently calculated, identified and processed. Programs scour image feeds looking for prescribed patterns of light and shade that correlate to its training set. The patterning of HyperFace is a new form of camouflage for this new machine world.

Hyphen-Labs and Adam Harvey,
HyperFace scarf prototype,
2017

right: When worn, the HyperFace scarf
distracts machine-vision algorithms
searching for a real human face by
creating a crowd of idealised faces.

below: The heat maps in this image outline
the regions of the pattern that trigger
high-level matches with the face detector's
training set. A frontal face-detector
algorithm is being tested, which is why
the most vertical faces are highlighted.

It is a visual subterfuge that operates less like traditional camouflage and more like a strategy of digital spoofing, creating a cloud of false positives. Our real face dissolves into a machine-readable crowd.

The HyperFace prototype is a computer-vision textile developed by Berlin-based American designer Adam Harvey and media art collective Hyphen-Labs for their NeuroSpeculative AfroFeminism (NSAF) project. 'Using fashion, cosmetics and the economy of beauty as entry points, the project illuminates issues of privacy, transparency, identity and perception,' writes Harvey.[1] The black-and-white pixel patterning on the HyperFace textile is generated from ideal algorithmic representations and proportions of a human face and designed to 'reduce the confidence score of facial detection and recognition by providing false faces that distract computer vision algorithms'.[2] If a machine is calibrated to see a world full of faces, then it is possible to exploit those expectations to generate a form of disappearance through diversion. It is a visual subterfuge that operates less like traditional camouflage and more like a strategy of digital spoofing, creating a cloud of false positives. Our real face dissolves into a machine-readable crowd.

To the human eye the HyperFace pattern is unrecognisable, a pixellated ground that is more a graphical equation than a mouth or pair of eyes. This is the beginning of an alternative graphic vocabulary with a form and materiality configured to anticipate the logics of computer perception rather than our own. A type of calibration graffiti, illegible in plain sight while signifying something highly specific to the machine lens. This is not decoration designed for us, this is ornamentation rooted in the emerging aesthetics of the Post-Anthropocene, where fashion cycles now follow the rate of Moore's Law, the latest phone model or software update rather than a change in natural season. Hyperface is a new visual language for a world where machines do the looking. ∆

The HyperFace scarf is a speculative product embedded within Hyphen-Labs' NeuroSpeculative AfroFeminism (NSAF) project, a transmedia exploration of black women and the roles they play in technology, society and culture.

To *the human eye the HyperFace pattern is unrecognisable, a pixellated ground that is more a graphical equation than a mouth or pair of eyes.*

Notes
1. See https://ahprojects.com/projects/hyperface/.
2. *Ibid.*

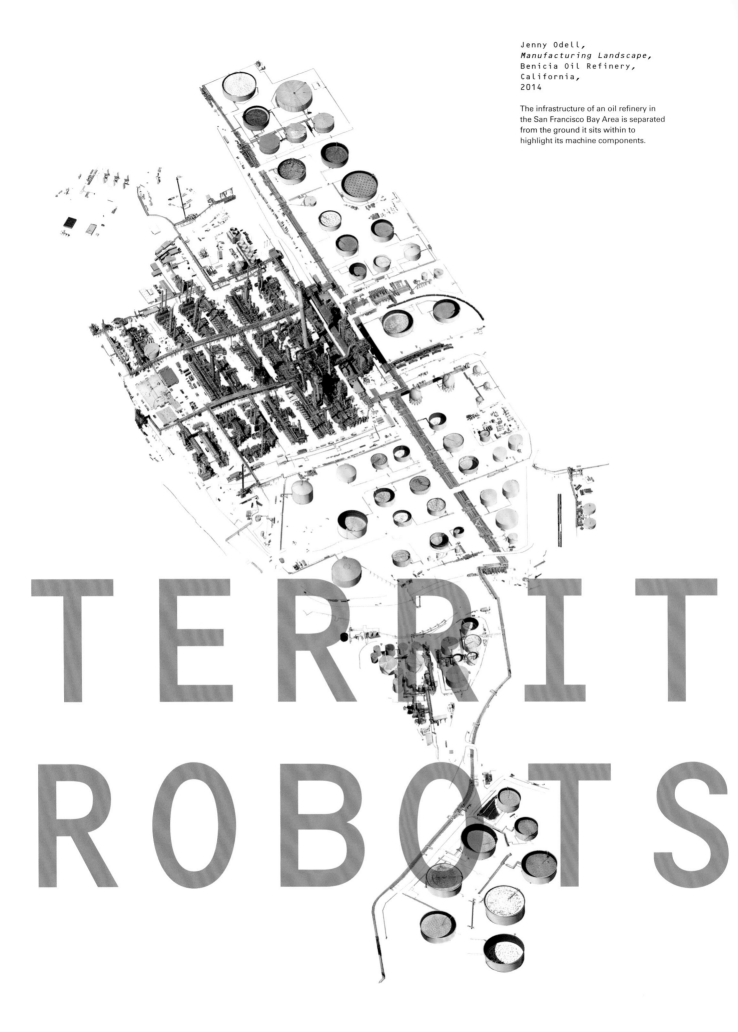

Jenny Odell,
Manufacturing Landscape,
Benicia Oil Refinery,
California,
2014

The infrastructure of an oil refinery in the San Francisco Bay Area is separated from the ground it sits within to highlight its machine components.

TERRIT
ROBOTS

Jenny Odell,
Power Landscape,
Palo Verde Nuclear Power Plant,
Tonopah,
Arizona,
2013

The systems and structures
of a nuclear generating station
as captured in satellite imagery.

Liam Young

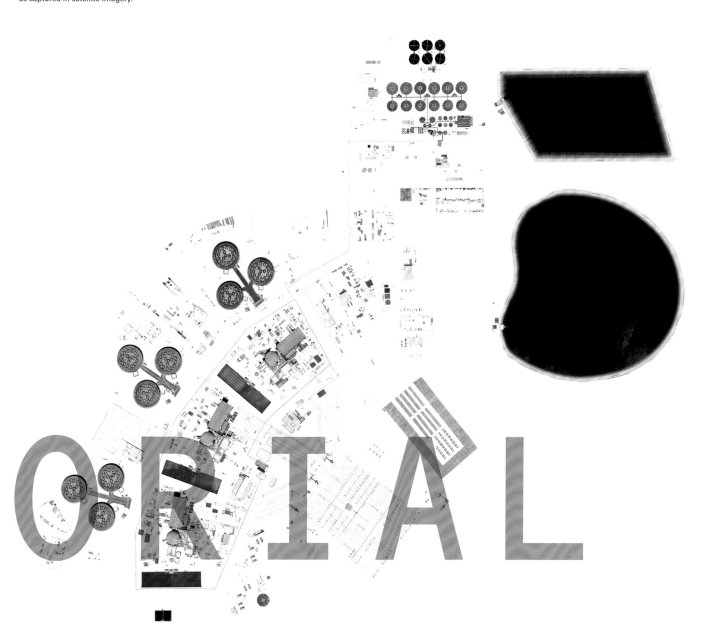

JENNY ODELL:
SATELLITE LANDSCAPES

In satellite photography, individuals on Earth are too small to be visible, yet our impact through technology is plain to see. American artist **Jenny Odell** tells Guest-Editor Liam Young how she has been scouring satellite imagery for industrial landscapes that serve as portraits by proxy, underlining our reliance on the machines we have created.

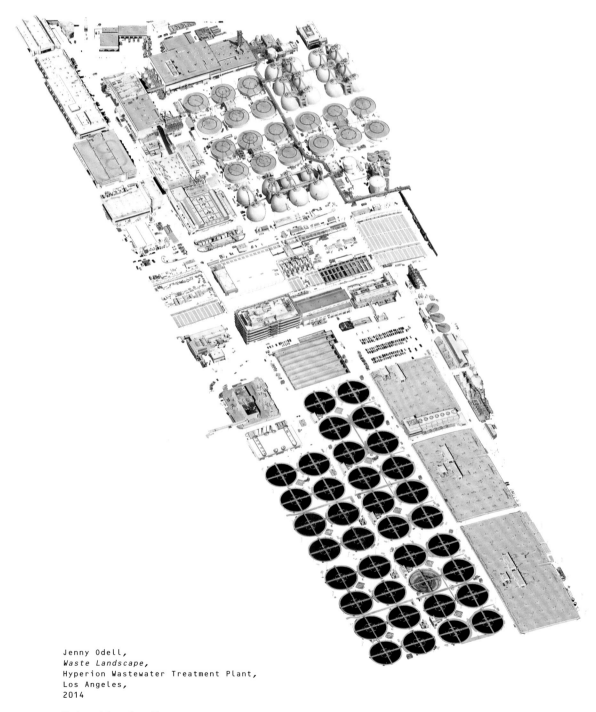

Jenny Odell,
Waste Landscape,
Hyperion Wastewater Treatment Plant,
Los Angeles,
2014

On the periphery of our cities are many forgotten landscapes like this one.

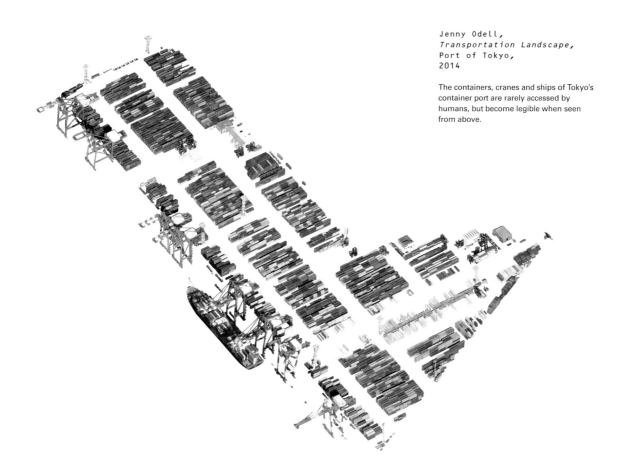

Jenny Odell,
Transportation Landscape,
Port of Tokyo,
2014

The containers, cranes and ships of Tokyo's container port are rarely accessed by humans, but become legible when seen from above.

Hurling around the earth at approximately 11,000 kilometres (6,835 miles) per hour is a flock of highly improbable machines. Delicately dancing with gravity, a group of satellite-mounted cameras look down on the world and tile together incredibly detailed photographs of its surface. These machine images constitute an archive that California-based artist Jenny Odell rummages through; as an archaeologist of the present she sifts through the dataset looking for traces of who we are and the mechanisms that sustain us. For Odell: 'The view from a satellite is not a human one, nor is it one we were ever really meant to see. But it is precisely from this inhuman point of view that we are able to read our own humanity, in all of its tiny, repetitive marks upon the face of the earth.'[1]

The intricate catalogues of machines that fill Odell's frames occupy the very periphery of our own territorial and psychological experience. For the most part the infrastructures that condition and construct our world have been rendered invisible to it. Disguised through distance, these are the landscapes around the back of the fridge, below the sink and under the hood. Odell's water treatment plants, mega container ports, power stations and resource fields sit behind chain-link fences, guard posts and remote coastlines, and it is only the orbiting lens of a satellite that allows us to see them as part of the continuous constructed fabric of our world. They are comfortably hidden away, unsung 'monuments' to an 'environmental irresponsibility' playing out at a terrifying scale.[2]

At the resolution of the satellite image, a pixel is slightly larger than the human body. At the scale of these infrastructures we do not register; we are just a discoloration, a dead pixel thoroughly embedded in the grain of technology and indistinguishable from the systems that surround us. We are not welcome in these sites, but the uncomfortable reality for a culture that does its best to ignore them is that they are central to the production of our urban environment. They are city machines, each drum and pipe, every connection and structure a critical component in the planetary-scaled robot that supports contemporary life. As Odell writes: 'If there is something unsettling about these structures, it might be that they are deeply, fully human at the same time that they are unrecognizably technological … They are our prostheses. They keep us alive and able, for a minute, to forget the precariousness of our existence here and of our total biological dependence on a series of machines, wires, and tubes, humming loudly in some far-off place.'[3] ⋈

Notes
1. See www.jennyodell.com/satellite.html.
2. www.jennyodell.com/satellite-landscapes.html.
3. *Ibid.*

Geoff Manaugh

INFRAST AS PROCESS

WH TO MO ARR TO

Cargo ship container terminal, Thailand

Automated marine port infrastructure brings together landscape-scale robotics with just-in-time distribution logistics to create labyrinthine environments where the human body is out-scaled spatially and outpaced temporally. The architectural features of these ports are minimal; these are not environments defined by fixed structures, but by complex spatial rules capable of near-real-time rearrangement. The port is automated space as scripted by shipping and storage algorithms.

RUCTURE
IONAL SPACE
ERE
RROW
IVES
DIAY

Yesterday's processional routes are in centres of human civilisation such as Rome. Today's are in environments that not only have no need for human presence, but require human absence in order to function. Yet the life of our great cities depends on such places. American writer **Geoff Manaugh** reports on his visit to a major marine transportation facility in Bayonne, New Jersey, where constantly shifting 'walls' of shipping containers are moved about by an algorithmically controlled mechanical system, with humans intervening only remotely and for mere seconds at a time.

The official slogan of the Global Container Terminals' marine transportation facility in Bayonne, New Jersey is 'Where tomorrow arrives today'.[1] Located due southwest of Manhattan, outside the boundaries of New York City, the terminal features 67 hectares (167 acres) of semi-automated cargo-processing space.[2] It is an open-air theatre of docks, cranes and gantries, an imposing orchestration of building-scale machines whirring away under limited human supervision, loading and unloading international container ships.

Backstage Pass

On an overcast afternoon in April 2015, I was able to tour the Bayonne facility alongside members of an organisation called the Infrastructure Observatory. To date, the Observatory, a private enthusiasts' group, has visited data centres, rail yards, Internet retail order-fulfilment warehouses and many other sites the explicit economic and technical purpose of which is to serve the metropolis while remaining metaphorically invisible or logistically out of sight.[3]

These facilities constitute a kind of peripheral commons, a shared, privately funded backstage for the realisation and maintenance of the contemporary city. They are the fringe that enables the centre, places where imports are scanned and stacked, where product subscriptions are fulfilled, and where other, often overlooked mundane services are performed for the benefit of a preoccupied citizenry. These are spaces of responsibility, responsible for supporting the everyday lives of consumers by responding to those consumers' most evanescent material needs.

For our tour of the Bayonne terminal, approximately a dozen people were in attendance, a demographically homogeneous mix of students, writers and professionals whose work in some way focused on logistics. There were software engineers and product-line managers, academic-historians and an amateur photojournalist. To see this range of interests projected onto semi-automated, towering walls of shipping containers, robotically relocated in near-real time according to temporary warehousing protocols, was an interesting glimpse of landscape interpretation at its most varied. While one attendee saw nothing more than helpful tricks for wholesale product stocking, another saw opportunities for recording oral histories of human labourers working amidst these machines that keep the fever dream of on-demand consumption alive.

Taken as a whole, the Bayonne site is a semi-automated interface, designed to ensure the frictionless transfer of goods from sea to land, and vice versa. 'All exit and entrance roads to the terminal are designed to keep the traffic flowing,' the site's promotional literature explains.[4] 'Dedicated transfer zones, pre-positioned cargo, and the elimination of cross-traffic intersections are just a few of the features that help keep operations running smoothly.' Indeed, the terminal highlights its economic value precisely as a spatial proposition, emphasising the site's proximity to nearby rail lines, bridges and turnpikes. Even its 'convenient location' on the New Jersey waterfront, as contrasted with nearby cargo terminals, is touted as having desirable temporal effects. It is geography, or space, repackaged as time.

Unknown Fields,
A World Adrift,
Hong Kong,
2014

top: Guest-editor Liam Young and architect Kate Davies run a programme with passing resemblance to the Infrastructure Observatory private enthusiasts' group. Unknown Fields, their nomadic studio, brings students, artists, writers and designers to sites of infrastructural interest around the world. For the World Adrift project the group visited a semi-automated marine port in Hong Kong.

above: The human figure is no more than an elusive presence in these mechanized landscapes, where humans are often tasked merely with supervising otherwise automated processes of loading and unloading or, ironically, with watching for moments of human error.

Space Oddity

Our guide to the terminal that afternoon pointed out that the clothes we were wearing, the cameras we had brought with us, even the pens and paper many of us were using to take notes, had probably entered the US through this very terminal. The remarks were a slightly ham-fisted philosophical reminder that all objects come from somewhere, as well as a thinly disguised attempt at self-promotion, positing lowly Bayonne as a gateway to New York City and beyond.

If Bayonne can be seen as the backstage of the Atlantic Seaboard, where global product flows are acquisitioned and arranged for their rapid distribution, then it was noteworthy that the terminal itself had its own backstage. This was the small core of human labourers, from blue-collar long-distance truck drivers to white-collar supervisors, who ensured that the port around them would continue to function as it should. Midway through the tour, for example, we entered the control room where human operators supervised the process of unloading cargo containers from docked ships. Giving the experience a note of unintentional

surreality, David Bowie's *Space Oddity* was playing on the office radio as we walked aisle to aisle, getting a first-hand glimpse of what role humans played in such a landscape.

That role, we soon learned, was minimal. Indeed, as Björn Henriksson, Technology Manager for the Swedish firm ABB Marine & Ports, has written, landscapes such as Bayonne are 'where human intervention is the exception'.[5] At Bayonne, human supervision was only required when one of the terminal's many industrial cranes came within 3 metres (10 feet) of a cargo container. It was only within this narrow spatial parameter that a human being was needed at all, and even this was performed through telepresence, using nothing more than a joystick and a closed-circuit television monitor. This framed a thoroughly indirect relationship to the landscape-scale robotics operating outside. What is more, these moments of human-assisted control lasted no more than 10 seconds apiece, after which the terminal's human operators were free to go back to whatever they had been doing previously – reading the paper, chatting about their weekend plans, or, as it happened, listening to David Bowie.

While it can be tempting to use architectural
analogies to describe the workings of these ports,
including the buttresses and naves of European
cathedrals, such comparisons fall short. These ports
function through an infrastructural density and
a rhythmic use of empty space that corresponds
purely to the logistical needs of vast pieces of
outdoor warehousing equipment.

Auto Schwarzenegger in Damage Land

At multiple times during our visit, it became clear that Bayonne's
exaggeratedly inhuman environment had inspired a number of
anthropological practices by which the port's human labourers
sought to orient and ground themselves. When one office-bound
operator reached the point where his crane went on autopilot, for
example, he referred to the software as 'Auto Schwarzenegger'. It
was a frivolous play on words, to be sure – a stupid joke – but it
was also an indication that, to help cope with the facility's faceless,
machinic nature, human characteristics had been projected onto
the equipment. 'Auto Schwarzenegger's got it now,' the man
muttered, releasing his joystick as the container disappeared
from screen. His monitor then simply went blank, making it clear
that the software thought the man had seen enough and that the
machines had taken over.

Outside, the relentlessly flat terminal landscape was jammed
with truck lanes and cargo containers, resembling an immersive
exercise in perspectival sculpture stretching to the horizon.
Despite this suggestion of visual clarity, the easily rearrangeable
labyrinth of containers standing around us was by no means easy
to navigate. Our own guide – who had been driving through these
same containers as recently as the day before – became disoriented,
looking out for landmarks that no longer existed and unable to
find his way back to the central office building.

This was true to the alarming extent that, at one point, we
actually found ourselves temporarily walled in by an unexpected
barrier four containers high, a kind of pop-up architectural feature
that, according to our guide, had not been there 24 hours earlier.
This confusing zone of shifting walls rearranged according to
algorithmic logics unavailable to human tourists was known
colloquially as 'Damage Land', our guide explained, another
humanist nickname for a depopulated area of ruined or damaged
containers awaiting refurbishment.

A human labourer engages with loading software he jokingly referred to by the
nickname 'Auto Schwarzenegger'. As soon as a target container is locked into place,
the worker's screen simply goes blank, implying that there is nothing else for
humans to see here – until the next container arrives, usually a minute or two later.

Global Container Terminals facility,
Bayonne,
New Jersey,
2015

The truck gates at the Bayonne facility are particularly significant examples of landscape-scale automation: before trucks can proceed into the facility, and before the robotically controlled equipment waiting above the gates can operate, the trucks' human drivers must exit their cabs and stand on pressure-sensitive pads. The message is clear: the human body is extraneous in this landscape, a potential risk whose presence must be surveilled and limited at all times.

The sight of more and more trucks awaiting entry into the terminal landscape felt not unlike watching a ceremonial gate at the periphery of some semi-sentient, maximum-security metropolis, a new kind of Forbidden City built not for humans but for machines.

Imprisoned in Ritual

It was here that we learned how strange a presence the human body could really be in an automated landscape such as this. At one of several truck entry gates, our guide explained that human drivers were required to get out of their vehicles and stand on a pressure-sensitive pad embedded in the ground. If a load approximating the driver's weight could not be detected by sensors, then the automated cranes above would not snap into motion. The landscape would remain dormant, frozen, useless, its efficient operation imperilled by human beings out of place.

This idea – that the presence of a human on a pressure-sensitive pad could activate a sequence of semi-autonomous machines waiting in the landscape around them – comes with multiple architectural implications, including a macabre glimpse of the future of the automated prison. Who needs guards when pressure-sensitive pads can simply lock or unlock unique paths of limited circulation for one individual only?

As we left, the sight of more and more trucks awaiting entry into the terminal landscape felt not unlike watching a ceremonial gate at the periphery of some semi-sentient, maximum-security metropolis, a new kind of Forbidden City built not for humans but for machines. The ceremonial use of urban space is often discussed in terms of papal processions through Rome or the ritualised passage of courtiers through imperial capitals in the Far East. However, the processional cities of tomorrow are already here and they are being run by algorithmic traffic-control systems and self-operating machines, in a thoroughly secular reinvention of ritual space, driven by automated protocols and sensor-controlled feedback networks.

To paraphrase Björn Henriksson, quoted earlier, in these cities human presence will be the exception. ∆

Notes
1. Global Container Terminals, Bayonne: http://globalterminalsbayonne.com/.
2. *Ibid.*
3. Infrastructure Observatory: http://infraobservatory.com/.
4. Global Container Terminals: http://globalterminalsbayonne.com/.
5. Björn Henriksson/ABB Marine & Ports, 'Automated Container Terminals are Taking Off': http://new.abb.com/marine/generations/technology/automated-container-terminals-are-taking-off.

The relentlessly flat semi-automated landscape of the Global Container Terminals cargo port in Bayonne hides the fact that the entire facility is organised around the efficient use of time. Algorithms guide the precise placement of individual containers even as the entire ensemble of cranes, truck gates, cargo stacks and ship-docking locations has been streamlined for rapid operations.

left: The interior of Amazon's logistics centre. Amazon employees are labelled as 'associates' by the corporation. 'Pickers' push trolleys around and pick out customers' orders from the aisles. They might each walk between 11 and 25 kilometres (7 and 15 miles) as part of their daily shift.

below: The efficiency of its huge warehouses is what enables Amazon to put parcels on customers' doorsteps so quickly.

A Place for Everything

Ben Roberts:
Amazon Unpacked

Amazon's warehouse, which looks like a huge blue box, is the size of nine football pitches and sits alongside a power station that dominates the town's skyline.

Amazon's warehouse shelves look chaotic – far from the orderliness of a traditional store or library. So how are our online orders fulfilled at such speed? Guest-Editor Liam Young reports on Madrid-based British photographer **Ben Roberts's** exploration of this environment governed by computer algorithms.

Workers in Amazon's warehouses (or 'associates in Amazon's fulfilment centres' as the company would put it) are divided into four main groups. There are the people on the 'receive lines' and the 'pack lines' who either unpack, check and scan every product arriving from around the world, or they pack up customers' orders at the other end of the process. Another group stows away suppliers' products somewhere in the warehouse.

Rugeley Power Station and the Amazon Fulfilment Centre, situated in close proximity to each other on the edge of the town.

Somewhere in Rugeley, a struggling former coal-mining town in the English Midlands, is a warehouse filled with everything. Amidst much community optimism the online shopping retailer Amazon has taken over a leftover site between a canal and a power station to construct the blank blue shell of one of its massive fulfilment centres. Like 'a smear of summer sky on the damp industrial landscape' it is an uncanny object, scaleless and out of place.[1] British documentary and travel photographer Ben Roberts journeyed behind the scenes of the Internet to rummage through the website's inventory and document the physical reality of one of the landscapes our clicks have built.

When we drag an item into our Amazon digital basket, on the other side of the screen a 'picker' in a bright-orange safety vest is rushing through these endless stacks, locating objects and dropping them into packing boxes. Each picker might walk up to 25 kilometres (15 miles) across their daily shift, constantly tracing the route through the building that is algorithmically generated for them by the personalised navigation tablets they all carry. Not a footstep is out of place, their paths optimised by proprietary sorting software and their bodies repurposed as a collection machine. 'You're sort of like a robot, but in human form … It's human automation, if you like,' says an Amazon manager.[2] Without this augmented orientation system, the nine football pitches of shelving appear as just a random assortment of impossibly jumbled objects. The markers of scale, distance and direction that would usually be found in such a landscape are totally absent and in most cases completely irrelevant. The Amazon bookshelves are not organised alphabetically or through the Dewey Decimal System, but are instead stacked based on a sorting algorithm engineered around sales frequencies and complex buying patterns. The search terms and suggested reading lists of Amazon crystallise into unintelligible juxtapositions and strategically calculated adjacencies.

Some of Amazon's fulfilment centres are now almost fully autonomous, the shuffling feet of pickers replaced by the smooth glide of mechanised robots. Other sites like this one, avoiding the cost outlay of an infrastructural overhaul, are still staffed by these human intruders, strangers amongst the dataset. The warehouse captured in Roberts's photography is a library for machines, a library that is not designed for us, an icon of the Post-Anthropocene, an early example of a new architectural typology that does not defer to our own patterns of orientation. This is a space organised by efficiency algorithms and inhabited by the human components of Amazon's global logistics robot. ⌀

Notes
1. Sarah O'Connor, 'Amazon Unpacked', *Financial Times*, 8 February 2013: www.ft.com/content/ed6a985c-70bd-11e2-85d0-00144feab49a.
2. *Ibid.*

HUMAN EXCLUSION ZONES

Jesse LeCavalier

LOGISTICS AND NEW MACHINE LANDSCAPES

Watson Land Company,
Still from promotional video
'Watson Reveals 36' Clear!',
2017

In warehouse real-estate, storage capacity is a primary concern. This still from a promotional video for Watson Land Company, a California developer, shows an additional 4-foot (1.2-metre) layer of storage added to a typical warehouse.

From automatically guided vehicles (AGVs) to robotic drive units (RDUs), warehouse operations have advanced apace in recent decades. **Jesse LeCavalier** – Assistant Professor of Architecture at the New Jersey Institute of Technology in Newark, and Daniel Rose Visiting Assistant Professor at the Yale School of Architecture in New Haven, Connecticut – recounts the development of the latest generation of adaptive, environment-reconfiguring machines, such as those created by Kiva Systems and its successor Amazon Robotics, and discusses their effect on architecture itself.

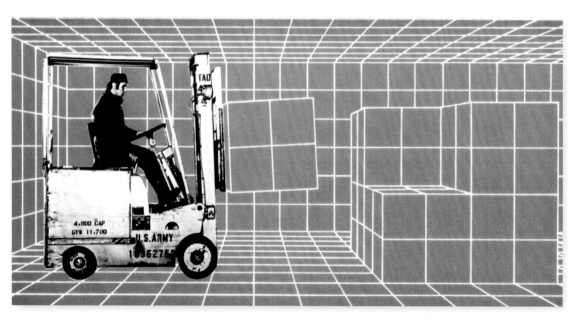

Charles B Einstein,
'Modeling the Wholesale Logistics Base',
Army Logistician,
November/December 1983

This illustration from *Army Logistician* describes a warehouse building's enclosure and its inventory in the same manner, suggesting they are conceptualised in similar terms.

One of the great stomachs of American consumerism sits east of Los Angeles, in the adjacent cities of Chino and Ontario. Processing and redirecting relentless quantities of inventory, this landscape encloses staggering amounts of 'cubic' feet – 'cube' in materials-handling argot. Architects might see this emphasis of volume (section) over area (plan) as a positive turn to experiential and spatial qualities. Materials-handling managers, however, see this simply as a question of capacity. These distribution and fulfilment zones create a machinic landscape all their own and one that, as it becomes more autonomous, poses challenges of both intelligibility and recognition to its human occupants.

Watson Land Company, one of the developers at work in Chino, distinguishes itself by offering a warehouse model that has a clear dimension from the top of the floor to the bottom of the ceiling of 36 feet (the more common height is 32). Multiply those 4 feet of height by one million square feet of area to understand what is at stake even in these small adjustments. A promotional video from 2014 (see the still on the previous spread) makes a case for choosing a warehouse with a 36-foot (10.9-metre) clearance by first introducing viewers to a digital model of a typical 32-foot (9.7-metre) example before a new 4-foot (1.2-metre) layer of blue 'cube' lands like a blanket of snow.[1] In the otherwise monochrome rendering of the warehouse, the envelope is left out, creating the impression that the racks, the ground and the trucks are all part of the same system. Though partly a product of visual necessity (it would be difficult to see the transformation of the 32-foot pallet racks otherwise), the choice resonates through the visual culture of materials handling and logistics because of a shared tendency to conflate the architecture with inventory or to omit it entirely.

For example, an image from the November/December 1983 issue of *Army Logistician* renders both warehouse interior and warehouse contents in the same fashion. The image's single-point perspective merges the gridded walls and floors with the stacked boxes of inventory and presages contemporary preoccupations with cubic feet by rendering generic inventory volume as physical substance. This material is made stackable and transportable through standardising functions necessary for the industries of logistics to operate. The storage pallet, for example, is a key element of standardisation because goods can be 'palletised' into rational units of measurement, a crucial step for the total management that came with the 'logistics revolution'.[2] This palletised unit of inventory has architectural implications because it has a physical dimension and so becomes a determining factor for warehouse construction.

In the *Army Logistician* image, all seems to be in its place except for the human forklift operator. The implied autonomy of a human operator is at odds with the otherwise regular logic of the warehouse environment. Indeed, the human aspect of logistics has resisted industry drives towards standardisation and automation even as the automatically guided vehicle (AGV) has emerged as a dominant attempt to overcome the expense and fallibility of human operations. Often serving specialised tasks and moving along fixed circuits, AGVs suggest a whole new set of organisational and spatial conditions.[3] Despite these technologies, the specific tasks of logistics, particularly the packing speed and picking dexterity required for assembling an order, continue to frustrate attempts at automation.

The Kiva system in use at a Gilt.com distribution centre, Shepherdsville, Kentucky, 2014

The Kiva robot system uses orange robotic drive units to deliver mobile inventory shelves to awaiting human pickers. Once the item has been picked, the shelf is returned to the closest available space.

Broadly speaking, the initial concerns of automation were primarily those of position, location and movement.[4] Early AGVs from the mid-1980s would follow fixed looping paths, often controlled by networks of transducers. By comparison, the system developed in the early 2010s by Mick Mountz and Kiva Systems does not require a predetermined path, but relies on a host of robotic drive units (RDUs) operating in unison and with common goals.[5] The RDUs go where they are needed and then return to the most convenient location. Kiva's innovation is significant because, despite numerous attempts, automated mobile fulfilment processes had not found a mainstream hold in the logistics industry. More typical approaches, by contrast, rely on fixed conveyors to move goods through a distribution centre. Automation still plays a significant role in these cases, but primarily in the sortation and routing of totes and packages. Humans walk (sometime miles in a day) to inventory locations to pick items and assemble an order before placing it on one of many automated belts.[6] Kiva's dramatic development, echoing EM Forster's *The Machine Stops* (1909), was to figure out a way to bring things to people instead of the other way around.[7] The Kiva system was purchased in 2012 by Amazon for $775 million and has become the cornerstone for the company's new venture, Amazon Robotics.

The small orange RDUs developed by Kiva are equipped with a threaded cam to lift inventory shelving units (pods) just enough to transport them to an available picking station and worker, all controlled by a warehouse management system (WMS). In order to have an item delivered for picking, a request is sent to all of the RDUs on the floor. According to the language of Kiva's patent, after this happens: 'The mobile drive units respond to the order request with bids that represent the amount of time each mobile drive unit calculates it would take to deliver the requested item.'[8] The 'winning' bid then delivers its charge to the awaiting station. Once the items have been picked, the RDU brings the shelf not to its original position, but to the closest open slot. Through this process, the warehouse is continuously reconfiguring itself.

Once the items have been picked, the RDU brings the shelf not to its original position, but to the closest open slot. Through this process, the warehouse is continuously reconfiguring itself.

A Kiva robotic drive unit in use
at an Amazon fulfilment centre,
DuPont,
Washington,
2015

The robotic drive units move the shelves by
lifting them slightly off the ground, reorganising
the building each time.

Kiva's breakthroughs were to granulise the system, to make storage and inventory the same thing, and to make storage mobile. Storage historically was often assumed to be a fixed element of distribution systems. Indeed, some storage racks serve double-duty as actual structural support for their building's roof system. In these cases, the storage becomes the architecture itself, fixed in place and stable. Kiva undoes this by not insisting that storage elements remain static and by animating them with a certain kind of intelligence. Instead of machine buildings populated with robot-like humans, as familiar science-fiction tropes might lead us to anticipate, Kiva creates a machine landscape of building-like robots.

The Kiva system's form of internal communication creates an overall organisation in which the racks with frequently requested items 'drift' closer to the packing stations. Mountz describes this as a 'complex adaptive system [that] demonstrates emergent system behaviour'.[9] His cites references like Steven Johnson's *Emergence: The Connected Lives of Ants, Brains, Cities* (2001) and Kevin Kelly's *New Rules for the New Economy: 10 Radical Strategies for a Connected World* (1998), texts also popular in architectural discourse, especially in the mid-2000s.[10] 'Emergence' and swarm behaviour remain tantalising for the discipline of architecture, and in this context Kiva's contribution is noteworthy because, rather than producing an image of a swarm, it uses small robots and pieces of buildings to create an actual emergent condition. Instead of a fixed form that suggests a field, here is a dynamic set of elements, each controlled by simple local feedback yet collectively creating a shifting whole whose form reflects a content we cannot understand. The map of a Kiva warehouse is a picture of our own collective consumer desires and impulsive quests for fulfilment, encrypted and presented back to us through a machine language that we cannot read. However, we would be mistaken to think that we are not part of this landscape.

Robotic drive units moving shelves around Amazon fulfilment centre,
Manchester,
2017

above: Amazon's robotic drive units occupy an exclusive part of its fulfilment centres in which they can move without interference from humans.

right: Amazon workers must check the inventory locations during the 'stowing' process. From there, the shelf will await delivery to a human picker who will select a product and add it to an order to be packed and shipped.

Once Amazon acquired Kiva, evidence of its activities became difficult to find. Amazon Robotics absorbed Kiva Systems and ended the sales of its products to other companies.[11] Since making Kiva part of its operations, Amazon has incorporated its technologies in a new generation of fulfilment centres that combine human picking, packing and shipping with automated inventory delivery. Much of the inventory is managed and processed in a multi-level area of each fulfilment centre known as the 'human exclusion zone'.[12] As goods arrive from suppliers they are 'stowed' in the inventory pods, which are then moved into the storage area. Since the RDUs get their directions from a grid of 2D barcodes on the ground, and since the local wireless network governs their location, the bots only need a small light to scan the codes on the floor. As a result, the human exclusion zone is dark. Dark and quiet. It is large enough that the rows of racks receding in the distance, when viewed from the outside, disappear into the blackness beyond. Periodically, an inventory pod on its way to a new location silently interrupts the long cross-aisles.[13]

Amazon has roughly 30,000 robotic drive units in operation and even though the company's automated fulfilment centres are increasingly full of machines, they remain part of a human condition. These buildings provoke a crisis of legibility in that we cannot understand the behaviour of their machines even though we created the instructions that guide them. When observing the RDUs in action, one is tempted to assign a kind of intelligence to these machines because they seem to operate with such unpredictable purpose. In 1984, the Italian cyberneticist Valentino Braitenberg created similar conditions by orchestrating a series of thought experiments in which simple 'vehicles' are assigned sensors (stimulus) and motors (response). By creating a series of mechanical feedback systems, apparent behaviours, emotions and even intelligence appear to emerge. Braitenberg posits that there is a tendency to conjecture that the vehicle 'does some thinking before it reaches a decision, suggesting complicated internal processes where in reality there was nothing but a threshold device waiting for sufficient activation. The patterns of behaviour described in the vehicles … undoubtedly suggest much more complicated machinery than that which was actually used in designing them.'[14] For him, more a psychologist than an engineer, the question is one of methodology and assumption; that sometimes to study something one needs to simulate its operations from the inside out. He reminds us that, 'when we analyse a mechanism, we tend to overestimate its complexity'.[15] And yet, while the operation of the individual RDUs is somewhat simple, the complexity that ensues over the 30,000 in Amazon's system suggests a different order of magnitude, one in which the individual vehicle is absorbed by a system with a propulsive technological force.

Architecture has always been a machinic landscape. Our challenge now is to offer suitably seductive responses, to proliferate typological inventions and to generate dispositional modes of practice that see the political problems of logistics as fundamentally architectural.

The apparent autonomy of the Amazon Robotics automated fulfilment centre floor suggests, if not creates, a sense of historical inevitability. The 'how' of the mechanism supersedes the 'why' and the spectacles of autonomous fulfilment landscapes justify the system that they propagate. In other words, the underlying assumptions and values about the consumer society upon which Amazon is built become more and more normalised through a set of technologies that creates greater and greater distance between action and consequences. Langdon Winner suggests that such technological momentum withers political agency because of the difficulty of comprehending systems beyond immediate experience: 'Most persons are caught between the narrowness of their everyday concerns and a bedazzlement at the works of civilization … With the overload of information so monumental, possibilities once crucial to citizenship are neutralized. Active participation is replaced by haphazard monitoring.'[16] In the case of Amazon, participation in a consumer process is rendered remote and instantaneous. We can 'track' the progress of our items, a process that reduces the efforts and complexities of the supply chain to a series of checkpoints. If we were to try to do more than 'haphazardly monitor' the process of order fulfilment, our frustration would continue because of the unintelligibility of the fulfilment landscape. A wilderness of machines of our own making that, while not autonomous, maintains a diffuse momentum of self-propagation.

Like electrification, fulfilment is on its way to becoming a new utility and a new expectation of contemporary life. And like electrification, it is changing us in the process. The degree to which we collectively depend on these systems then becomes a key question. In the context of an increasingly technomorphic landscape, companies like Amazon thrive if we are isolated as individual consuming subjects. But in that isolation, to return to Winner: 'Seemingly valid excuses can be manufactured wholesale for anyone situated in the network. Thus the very notion of moral agency begins to dissolve.'[17] If we accept that automation has a technological momentum that will work to shape the built environment to its own expedient ends then, rather than stepping aside to let technology run its course, there is an opportunity to treat this as an architectural issue, or at least as a spatial one. Architecture has always been a machinic landscape. Our challenge now is to offer suitably seductive responses, to proliferate typological inventions and to generate dispositional modes of practice that see the political problems of logistics as fundamentally architectural. ∆

NOTES
1. 'Watson Reveals 36' Clear!', Watson Land Company promotional video: https://youtu.be/H3P8d1_pVgg.
2. W Bruce Allen, 'The Logistics Revolution and Transportation', *Annals of the American Academy of Political and Social Science*, 553, September 1997, pp 101–16.
3. Keller Easterling, *Floor*, in Rem Koolhaas/AMO/ Harvard Graduate School of Design (eds), *Elements*, Marsilio Editori (Venice), 2014.
4. John Harwood, 'Architectures of Position', in Lluís Alexandre Casanovas Blanco et al, *After Belonging: The Objects, Spaces, and Territories of the Ways We Stay in Transit*, Lars Müller (Zurich), 2016, pp 226–33.
5. Michael C Mountz, 'Material Handling Method Using Autonomous Mobile Drive Units and Movable Inventory Trays', US Patent 6,748,292 B2, 8 June 2014: https://patentimages.storage.googleapis.com/cf/19/af/ f4db8f47c28bd0/US6748292.pdf.
6. John Cassidy, 'Amazon and the Realities of the "New Economy"', *The New Yorker*, 19 August 2015: www.newyorker.com/news/john-cassidy/amazon-and-the-realities-of-the-new-economy.
7. EM Forster, 'The Machine Stops', first published in the *Oxford Cambridge Review*, 1909: http://archive. ncsa.illinois.edu/prajlich/forster.html.
8. Mountz, *op cit*.
9. *Ibid*.
10. Steven Johnson, *Emergence: The Connected Lives of Ants, Brains, Cities*, Scribner (New York), 2001. Kevin Kelly, *New Rules for the New Economy: 10 Radical Strategies for a Connected World*, Penguin (New York), 1998. For examples of the discussion of emergence in architecture, see for instance Michael Hensel, Achim Menges and Michael Weinstock, ∆ *Emergence: Morphogenetic Design Strategies*, May/ June (no 3), 2004, pp 6–10.
11. See 'Supply Chain News: Amazon Will Not Make Kiva Systems Available to General Market for at Least Two Years', *Supply Chain Digest*, 31 March 2014: www.scdigest.com/ontarget/14-03-31-1.php?cid=7944, and Kim Bhasin and Patrick Clark, 'How Amazon Triggered a Robot Arms Race', *Bloomberg Business Week*, 29 June 2016: www.bloomberg.com/news/ articles/2016-06-29/how-amazon-triggered-a-robot-arms-race.
12. Nick Wingfield, 'As Amazon Pushes Forward With Robots, Workers Find New Roles', *New York Times*, 10 September 2017: https://www.nytimes. com/2017/09/10/technology/amazon-robots-workers. html.
13. Based on a tour of the Amazon EWR4 facility in Robbinsville, New Jersey, 19 September 2017.
14. Valentino Braitenberg, *Vehicles: Experiments in Synthetic Psychology*, MIT Press (Cambridge, MA), 1986, p 21.
15. *Ibid*, p 20.
16. Langdon Winner, *Autonomous Technology: Technics-out-of-Control as a Theme in Political Thought*, MIT Press (Cambridge, MA), 1989, p 296. First published 1977.
17. *Ibid*, pp 303–4.

John Gerrard,
Farm (Pryor Creek, Oklahoma),
2015

After being denied access to visit the Google Data Farm, Gerrard took to the skies in a small helicopter to photograph the building from above.

Liam Young

Where the Internet Lives

John Gerrard: *Farm*

John Gerrard,
*Farm
(Council Bluffs, Iowa),*
2015

The primary function of the
architecture is to condition and
move air at the right temperature
through the stacks of servers it
holds inside.

Gerrard's images are devoid of
any people. The infrastructure
of the Internet does not need
human inhabitants and does
not encourage visitors.

The digitised data farm slowly
changes from day to night
across the course of Gerrard's
animation. In the darkness it is
bathed in industrial floodlights.

John Gerrard,
Farm (Pryor Creek, Oklahoma),
2015

above: Built from repetitive modules and
components, the data farm can be
extended indefinitely, always growing
to accommodate our culture's dataset.

right: The anonymity of Google's building
disguises the extraordinary technology
and cultural archive that is housed within.

The Cloud is not just floating in the ether – it has several physical homes. Humans rarely set foot in these ultra-high-security, alien settings, yet they are central to our culture today. Guest-Editor Liam Young describes how Irish artist **John Gerrard** used photographs taken from a helicopter to conjure a virtual tour of them.

In an anonymous town in Oklahoma is one of the largest cultural landscapes in human history. Housed within a cluster of blank warehouses are the endless rows of server stacks and processors that now contain everything about who we are. All of our images, books, music, inane chatter, dreams and fears, histories and futures are here, drowning in the constant whir of cooling fans. Terms like 'cloud', 'wifi' and 'web' are suggestive of something omnipresent, ephemeral, everywhere and nowhere, yet this network is organised around an extraordinary planetary-scaled physical infrastructure. If you were to yank your Internet cable from the wall and follow this loose thread you may eventually find yourself standing in this unremarkable part of the world surrounded by the rumbling machines that form Google. These are the Google Data Farms and they are where the Internet lives.

In 2014 Irish artist John Gerrard tried to get access to visit a number of these sites, but was denied by Google Inc. With no other means of access, he hired helicopters to fly above the sprawling complexes and document them through meticulous aerial photography. For his subsequent project *Farm*, a team of modellers and computer-graphics artists worked with him to transform these 2D images into a precise, hyper-realistic 3D model of the inaccessible site. By importing the finished models into game engine software, the artist was able to generate animations of his own revealing journeys around buildings he had never set foot within. Rows of cooling towers, banks of diesel generators, aluminium-clad sheds and manicured lawns form the unassuming exterior of a machine landscape that should be so intimate to all of us.

Gerrard's unsettling tour of these infrastructural ghosts raises the question of how sites like these should be understood within our culture. While they are rarely physically accessed by humans, the contents of these buildings are deeply personal and touched by all of us. For some the data centre is a site for proprietary machines, for the efficient storage and processing of information, and for others it is a site of pilgrimage, a public territory, an entity that owes us access. The Google Farm is not a great library or a grand cathedral, but when our collective history is digital, this is our generation's cultural legacy. It is a world of information trapped behind a disclosure agreement, a formless facade and a security-patrolled tank-proof fence. ₪

Rem Koolhaas, OMA

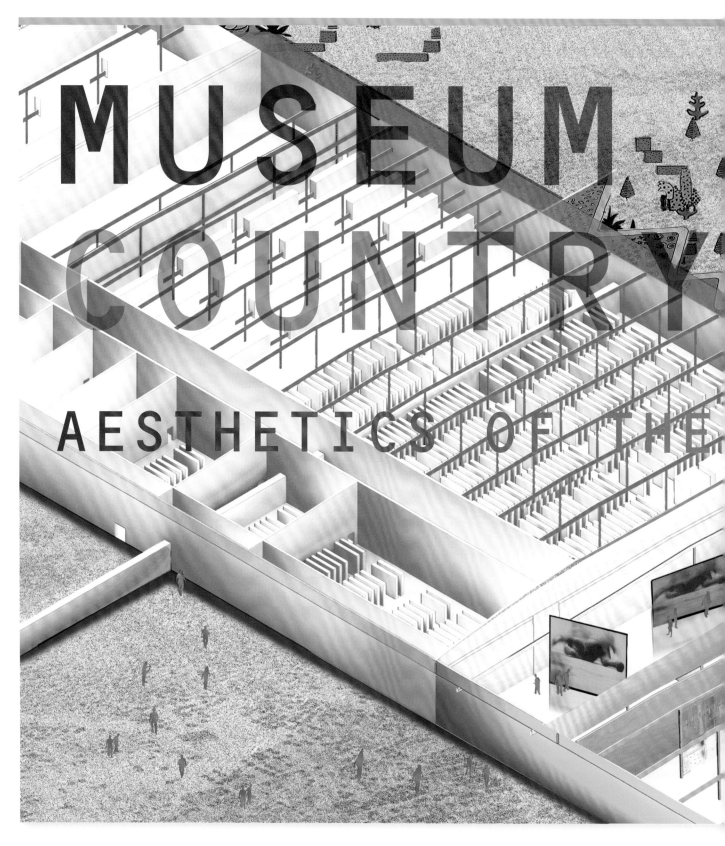

MUSEUM COUNTRY
AESTHETICS OF THE

OMA,
Museum in the Countryside,
2018

At a moment when our collective history is digital, the
data centre is becoming one of our most significant
cultural typologies. In this context the spaces of museum
storage and experience are afforded new relevance in
what would have once been an unexpected alliance.

IN THE
SIDE
DATA CENTRE

As part of OMA's forthcoming exhibition 'Countryside: Future of the World', which opens at the Solomon R Guggenheim Museum in New York this autumn, the office is cataloguing the emergence of a new kind of architecture, the data centre. These vast, monolithic facilities are not designed to be inhabited by humans, but through their unimaginable scale and radical starkness they illicit the sensibilities of a new technological sublime. OMA founder **Rem Koolhaas** explores the ways through which architects might be able to engage this condition through cultural programmes and make it accessible to the people it would otherwise exclude.

As architects, we have been involved in thinking about museums at OMA since the late 1980s. One of the issues that preoccupies us is how – in the age of massive artworks and enormous visitor numbers – to maintain the authenticity of the encounter between the artwork and the visitor. How can certain techniques, technologies, radical new combinations and new contexts benefit and stimulate our experience of the museum?

In 1997, in a competition for the Museum of Modern Art (MoMA) in New York, we proposed for the first time a view-on-demand system for artworks. Individual visitors, with individual desires, could see the museum potentially more as an archive of things than a place where the voice of curator is paramount. The idea was not only about generating unique personal experiences of particular artworks; it was about merging storage and display in one integrated system. When you see some of the works in any museum's storage facilities, it is a crying shame that they are not accessible to the public. For many institutions, the idea of leaving so many works in storage has been an incentive, especially in the last 20 years, to constantly expand their museums. Funding and philanthropy becomes focused on architectural expansion at the expense of less tangible functions. Tate Modern at Bankside in London now has a new wing, which is basically bigger; the argument is we can show bigger works from mediums that require more space. The Pompidou in Paris has an outpost, but again the argument is that it is bigger.

As architects we are constantly wondering where architecture is going and how relevant it is. Museums are under similar pressure, yet constantly repeat the same formula. Why is there not more adjustment and more creativity on every level, from physical conception to programming? If you look at the typology of museums, there is stagnation.

This is where OMA's interest in museums potentially intersects with another preoccupation – the countryside. At some point we became aware that typically urban conditions are being used to declare what architecture is becoming. But we had an instinct that it was more interesting to look at the countryside, the non-urban condition, where more urgent transformations are taking place.

The urban surface of the world is only 2 per cent, yet there is very little thought among architects about the other 98 per cent. It is strange that so much territory can be outside our vision. Countryside is now completely different from our nostalgic notions, impacted and conditioned by connectivity of all kinds. Digital surveillance covers almost every square inch of the world and creates a vast increase in knowledge of things we never see. This is clearly a paradox: we do not go to the countryside any more, but theoretically we know more about it than ever before. The digital is perhaps used more to affect the non-urban condition than the urban one.

And the countryside is where this digital power emanates and is stored. Looking at the countryside today, there is an emergence of a new kind of architecture, the aesthetic of the data centre. You could be upset that huge facilities are appearing across such beautiful landscapes, unimaginably massive, inert boxes seemingly lacking 'architectural' qualities. These spaces are not intended to be inhabited; they are hardly even meant to be used or experienced by

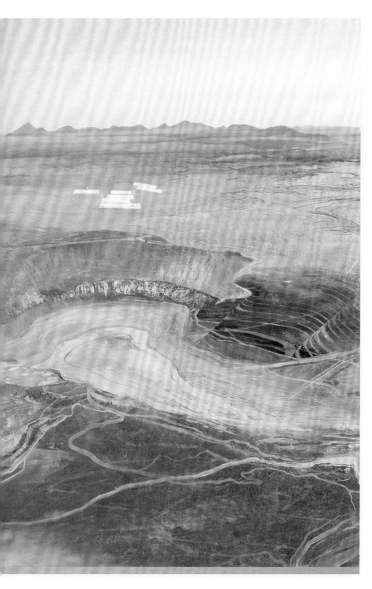

opposite: Set among the rectilinear slabs of the countryside data centre, the bays of the museum extend the formal arrangement of the server stacks and seamlessly connect to the existing building services infrastructure.

below: Seen from the air, the data centre museum reads as stark, unadorned figures in the landscape.

The conditions for the archiving and experience of art are efficiently aligned with the cooling requirements and stable air necessary for the optimal functioning of server stacks.

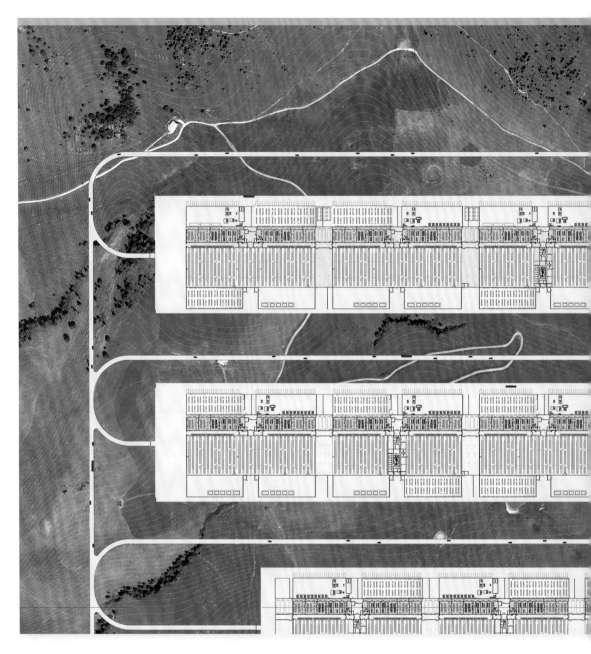

The spaces of the data centre are almost entirely devoid of people. As human occupants are retreating from the countryside, the museum programme would reoccupy the landscape with a new form of public activity.

human beings. Nevertheless, or maybe because of that, they are outrageously beautiful and new, almost the definition of the sublime – as something producing an overwhelming sense of awe or other high emotion through being vast, grand. Once you look at these facilities with a Land Art sensibility, their physical dimensions and the activities within are surprisingly artistic as well as utilitarian. As architects, we are asking: can you modify or add something to that situation, to make it explicit, coherent and accessible to the people it otherwise excludes?

The proposition is to use the architectural configuration of the data centre for a museum, almost without any change. We do not know whether this is impossible. Data centre architecture operates on the purest form of a grid; you maintain the same grid and use it as a place where storage and exhibition can coexist (data and art are both forms of storage).

Such a museum would automatically benefit from a deep analogy between industrial work and artistic realisation. It could introduce multiple activities that may never have been combined before: the conservation not only of works held by the museum, but also for the work of collectors, private institutions and corporations; viewing on demand; auctions, events, exhibitions; even the testing of exhibitions in different configurations or with different curatorial parameters – a facility that no major museum currently has at its disposal.

By moving the museum to the countryside, a completely new and unexpected situation is immediately created, in a context where there is a global curiosity but little knowledge. The museum would become an articulation of public activity where only data storage is proliferating, a function by necessity devoid of people.

What is really exciting is that this is an architecture where the ego of the architect is completely absent. It is based on a reading of the future for any cultural institution, but also on the emerging coexistence between technologies and human beings, articulated in the context of art. The purity of intention, undistorted by architectural vision, is what is particularly attractive about this possibility. ⌀

The rigid bays of the data centre typology house both the regimented rows of 19-inch server stacks and the climate-controlled spaces of museum archiving and visitor experience.

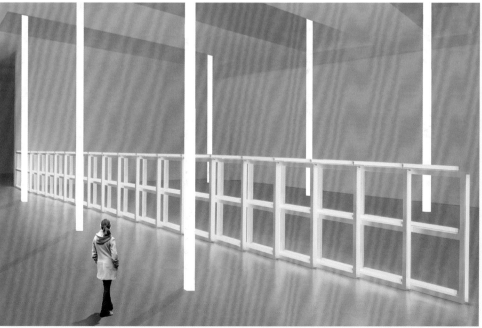

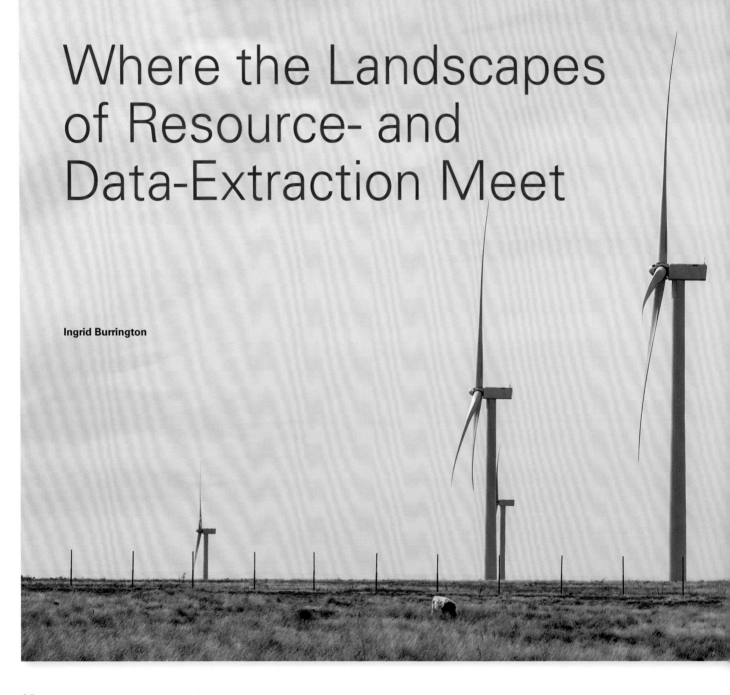

A Benediction Amazon Wind

Where the Landscapes of Resource- and Data-Extraction Meet

Ingrid Burrington

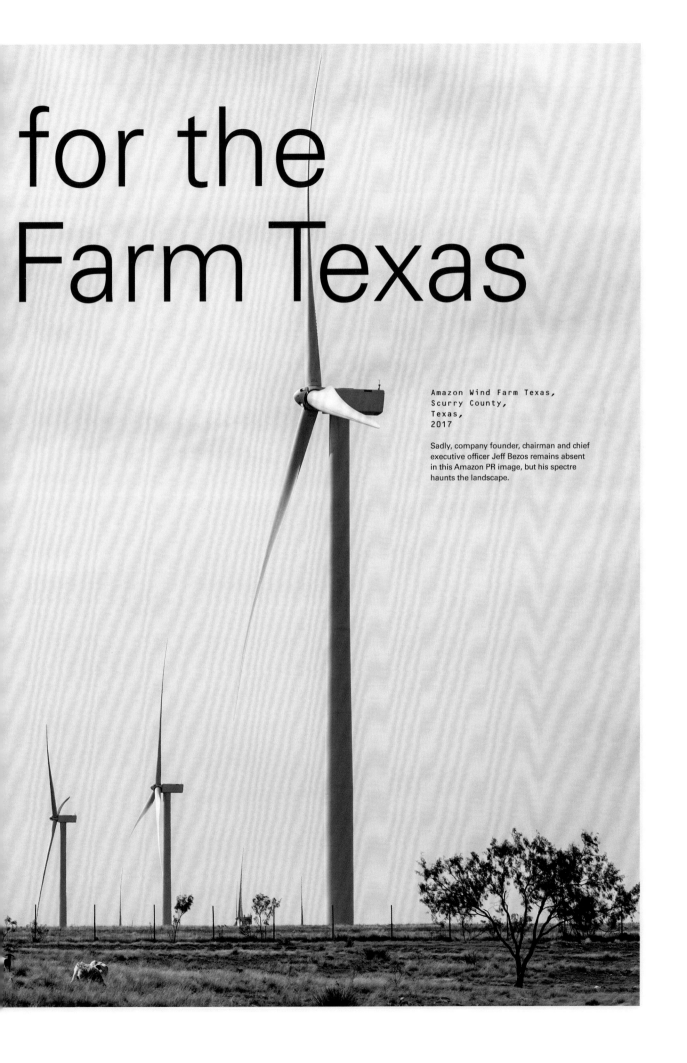

for the Farm Texas

Amazon Wind Farm Texas,
Scurry County,
Texas,
2017

Sadly, company founder, chairman and chief executive officer Jeff Bezos remains absent in this Amazon PR image, but his spectre haunts the landscape.

Our online activities can have a hefty carbon footprint. Some of the big tech companies have been taking responsibility for this by investing in sustainable energy projects. Having visited the site of Amazon's first wind farm, New York-based writer and artist **Ingrid Burrington** questions the motivations and outcomes of such ventures.

Somewhere near the future home of Amazon Wind Farm Texas, outside of Snyder, Scurry County, Texas, 2017

Scurry County already has a number of large operational wind farms.

I had come to Texas in bad faith and with worse timing, and I knew it. This truth, one which unfortunately defined many of my sojourns into geographies of network infrastructure, sunk in clearly as I stood to the side of the road on a state highway staring at a too-empty horizon. Somewhere, within my line of sight lay the future home of Amazon's next massive wind farm project. I was too early. It was February, the project had been announced that past September, and the few signs of construction were too minute to be seen from my vantage point. They might have been somewhere reachable via a gated dirt road that I had chosen not to attempt in my already-worn rental car. While the gate was clearly easy to scale on foot, trespassing charges simply for the possibility of seeing the groundwork of an eventual energy behemoth seemed a bit much.

The 253-megawatt Amazon Wind Farm Texas would be officially completed eight months later, in October 2017. Upon its completion, Amazon released a video of company founder, chairman and chief executive officer Jeff Bezos standing atop one of its industrial turbines, a bottle of christening champagne in hand and a hard-hat atop his usually gleaming bald head. The image of Bezos smashing the bottle against the turbine as the camera zoomed out to reveal blades roughly the wingspan of a Boeing 747 marks the moment that his calculated public image began to make affordances for swagger – if not a sense of humour, then at least an acknowledgement that wealth was treating the man well. It was also the company's biggest gesture towards sustainability and corporate social responsibility, topics that Amazon had strenuously avoided for years, but apparently could either no longer afford to ignore or could now instrumentalise as part of a much-needed public relations campaign.

Amazon Wind Farm Texas, Scurry County, Texas, 2017

This image of the Amazon Wind Farm Texas is characteristic of the stock-photo genre of 'charismatic mega-infra', valorising and visualising infrastructure absent of its human labour and political economy.

Cleaning Up the Cloud

Amazon is not the only big-tech company to invest in wind farms – it is actually pretty late to the game. In 2012, when Greenpeace began a multi-year campaign to call out the 'dirty clouds' of coal-powered data centres, companies like Google, Facebook and Microsoft sprang into action to clean up their computational carbon footprint. The preferred mechanism for this cleanup were power purchase agreements (PPAs), contracts arranged with regional electricity providers to invest in the construction of renewable-energy sources in exchange for low fixed power costs for a set number of years. Rather than directly constructing a power source solely dedicated to the data centre, PPAs allow companies two convenient if contradictory narratives. First, the company's carbon footprint is 'offset' by the introduction of this renewable power source. Second, through the benevolence of investing in the regional power grid rather than some standalone project directly connected to the data centre, companies generously serve the community with renewable energy. Because the movements of electrons in a power grid are not as easily tracked as bits of data on a server blade, Amazon, Google and Facebook can rest easy in this paradoxical framing of individual carbon-neutrality and community-minded sustainability investment.

The first phase of Amazon's wind farm in Texas, for instance, can power up to 90,000 homes,[1] which is another way of saying that some minute fraction of Amazon's electricity needs for its data centres is equal to the power use of 90,000 homes. Carbon neutrality apparently also neutralises critique, as such announcements tend to bypass the question of to what end companies expend so much computational power and whether such an energy expenditure is even necessary.

Data centres in the making are a lot easier to find than wind farms in the making: the former are smaller, more contained and generally subject to more Googleable public documentation (permits, planning documents and so on). It was ostensibly a data centre tour that brought me to Texas – or, rather, the insistent PR representative of a mid-tier Dallas data centre company, under the mistaken impression they were journalistically compelling and that I was professionally useful to them. But the wind farm some 420 kilometres (260 miles) away in Scurry County was a bigger draw, I thought. I contrived some reasons to drive from Dallas to El Paso, insisting the wind farm was conveniently 'on the way' (it was, in fact, two and a half hours out of the way).

Papalote Creek Wind Farm,
Taft, Texas,
March 2018

Located about 32 kilometres (20 miles) from Rockport, Texas, where Hurricane Harvey first made landfall in 2017, Papalote Creek was the first wind farm in the US to face the test of Category 4 hurricane winds.

Landscape of Texas oil infrastructure alongside wind turbines. Texas currently generates more wind energy than Iowa, Oklahoma and California combined, and in 2017 produced 1.2 billion barrels of oil.

Even the Wind is Bigger in Texas

The route to El Paso cut across the heart of the Permian Basin, an ancient sediment formation spanning some 400 kilometres (250 miles) and the largest petroleum-producing basin in the US. It is still a pretty active region for oil prospecting. Reminders of the industry litter Interstate 20 – hulking compounds of machinery presumably used for something important and heavy, rows of tanker trucks glimpsed out of the corner of the eye, oil derricks bobbing like bored birds in a pond. Wind turbines, more often associated with killing birds than metaphorical comparisons to them but in similarly stalwart flocks, also dotted the landscape. Despite its reputation as a stronghold of climate change denial, Texas is the largest producer of wind energy in the US, and the construction of wind farms has brought reliable jobs (and income in the form of leasing private farmland) to a part of rural west Texas otherwise subject to the economic vacillations of the oil industry. Aerial and satellite imagery illustrates the wind boom with less elegance than the solemn sentries of white turbines on the interstate horizon: turbines, and the makeshift roads between them, spiral out onto the landscape like more drunken scrawling than Nazca lines.

This abundance is, in part, why Amazon built a wind farm in Texas, where it lacks a data centre footprint. The company might have also chosen Texas because it was planning ahead. Over the past four years, the Dallas-Fort Worth region has positioned itself as a central data centre hub, owing to an abundance of fibre-optic cable routes, cheap land and cheap energy. Facebook finished construction of a $1 billion data centre in Fort Worth in 2016 (also wind powered); other companies have followed suit. There is a facile inevitability to this. Of course a region so defined by the extractive regimes of oil would give way to the extractive regimes of data, a gossamer abstraction all-too-often heralded as the 'new oil', extraction wiped clean of the violence and climate change implications of the methods preceding it (assuming, of course, one ignores all toxic industrial mining necessary to manufacture computers, and petroleum necessary to produce and refine chemicals for the same purpose).

Aerial imagery of Snyder and its surrounding wind farms,
Scurry County, Texas,
September 2016

While Snyder remains in many respects an oil town, the
significant impact of wind energy (emanating from centre right)
on the landscape is abundantly clear viewed from a distance.

The Foreclosed Futures of Infrastructure Computing

This misunderstanding of data as a pure resource rather than reliant on resources is one that Bezos himself embraced. In an interview published in Brad Stone's *The Everything Store: Jeff Bezos and the Age of Amazon* (2013), Bezos explicitly compared his vision for Amazon Web Services (AWS) to an electrical power grid: 'As soon as the electric power grid came online, [factories] dumped their electric power generator, and they started buying power off the grid. It just makes more sense. And that's what is starting to happen with infrastructure computing.'[2]

Bezos's vision for AWS assumes a reality where the power grid – and access to energy resources for powering it – are already solved problems. As the company's data centre footprint (and public scrutiny of it) has grown, this fantasy has partially dissolved into the pragmatic pursuit of PPAs, investment in substations, and the strategic construction of data centres in regions where electricity and water are cheap and plentiful. But like most acts of corporate social responsibility, these sustainable data centre initiatives seem more designed to abdicate liability. It moves the question of whether the tremendous energy overhead of complex computation at scale is worth its social and environmental costs into the feel-good promise of wind farm investments and 90,000 homes powered, or 90,000 cycles powered, or maybe both as the reality of how power grids actually work renders distinction meaningless. In greater contradiction, these energy investments also lend coherence to tech platforms' insistence that they, too, are infrastructure in the heavy and utterly indispensable sense of the word. Like a nation constructed around highways prematurely foreclosed on a future not defined by petroleum, the entrenching and carbon-cancelling of the data centre forecloses on the possibility of questioning whether so much of this computational future is even necessary.

Like a nation constructed around highways prematurely foreclosed on a future not defined by petroleum, the entrenching and carbon-cancelling of the data centre forecloses on the possibility of questioning whether so much of this computational future is even necessary.

In West Texas, old and new extractive landscapes collapse into each other in an easy coexistence. Data is not here to replace oil; it merely evades association and culpability with its less desirable consequences. The real bad faith and bad timing of my journey might have been believing that there may still be time to outrun or engineer a way out of these futures predicated on extraction. Δ

Notes
1. Day One Staff, 'Amazon Launches Largest Wind Farm Yet', 19 October 2017: https://blog.aboutamazon.com/sustainability/amazon-launches-largest-wind-farm-yet.
2. Brad Stone, *The Everything Store: Jeff Bezos and the Age of Amazon*, Little, Brown (New York), 2013, p 221.

TENDING GOATS AND MICROPROCESSORS

Liam Young

XINGZHE LIU: UNCOVERING SICHUAN'S REMOTE BITCOIN MINES

A new technological industry is stirring deep in rural China: Bitcoin mines operated by hydroelectric power from mountain streams. Photojournalist **Xingzhe Liu** took the long hike to discover their operators' working conditions. Guest-Editor Liam Young relays the dark and gruelling tale of what he found.

Xingzhe Liu,
Bitcoin mine,
Ngawa Tibetan and Qiang
Autonomous Prefecture,
Sichuan province,
China,
2016

above: Cooling fans draw air inside an unfinished building to air condition the array of processors at the remote Bitcoin mine.

right: A 29-year-old man operates a rig of Bitcoin mining machines on behalf of other miners who do not want to move to rural Sichuan. A wall of cooling fans has been built to keep the machines operating at their optimal temperature.

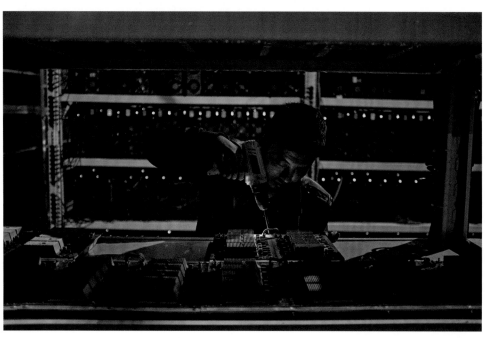

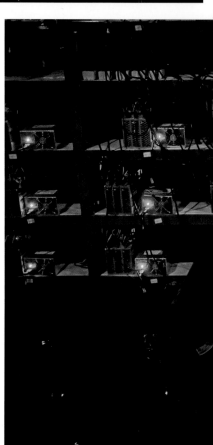

above: A worker puts together a used circuit board and adds it to the processing array at the Bitcoin mine. Seven employees work in shifts monitoring the machines to keep the mine running 24 hours a day.

right: A worker inspects a malfunctioning mining machine during his night shift. Miners can check a machine's condition and operations using phones and personal computers. For most issues they can simply restart a machine.

The relationship between goats and bitcoins is not immediately apparent. Amidst the death throes of late capitalism, however, such incongruities seem to thrive. In the remote mountain regions of Sichuan province, China, a herd gathers beside the cooling fan of a cryptocurrency mine. They have wandered in from a nearby farm; they know nothing of the complex mathematical equations that are being solved on the other side of the wall by stacks and stacks of hastily soldered-together processing boards, but they can certainly recognise a cool breeze. Until recently, local economies have been focused around goat herding and agriculture. Now, cheap hydroelectric power drawn from high-altitude rivers has set in motion a new industry of computation.

Rather than the blind faith we invest in the culturally constructed value of yellow rocks, Bitcoin is a currency that ultimately derives its worth from energy. It requires electricity to run the calculations that generate new coins, and these processes have found a new natural home among the electricity plants scattered along the region's mountain streams. If you have ever bought or traded bitcoins then chances are they were mined here in China. Local photo-journalist Xingzhe Liu trekked along the riverbanks to visit the currency machines and meet the miners who man the racks of rumbling microprocessors. This clandestine industry operates across a loose collection of legal regulations, so Liu is careful not to mention the names of mining villages or the full names of the miners themselves.

Here, massive warehouses are filled not with factory workers, but with networked computers running 24 hours a day. These are not the dust-free clean rooms of Western tech companies, but the sweaty, crammed and tangled shelves of an unregulated rural boom town. Entire rooms are stuffed with component packaging, quickly ripped off a new unit before it is wired into the line. Human workers tend to the machines, sleeping in dormitories and fixing any processors that go offline. For the most part they sit on their phones, drifting the Web, waiting for a machine to go down and the call to action. Just like an agricultural worker tending the field, they monitor their crops, green LEDs flickering, waiting for harvest. This is the front line of cryptocurrencies, not the hipster bedrooms or startups of California. Among the clouds and the goats of remote Sichuan, the machine landscapes of cutting-edge global finance keep on whirring. ♌

This is the front line of cryptocurrencies, not the hipster bedrooms or startups of California.

Merve Bedir and Jason Hilgefort

FRINGES OF TECHNOLOGY AND SPACES OF ENTANGLEMENT IN THE PEARL RIVER DELTA

Huaqiangbei District, Shenzhen, 2017

One of the biggest electronics markets in the world, shining advertisements into the streets around.

China's Pearl River Delta is a burgeoning megalopolis and a hotbed of technological transformation. Based in one of its cities, Shenzhen, the spatial knowledge exchange platform Aformal Academy was set up to explore the nature of this transformation. Its co-founders **Merve Bedir** and **Jason Hilgefort** present a range of ventures that have been happening on the urban and digital margins, where human and nonhuman intermingle. Mechanisation, e-commerce, online supply-chain management and data harvesting are impacting a whole array of fields, from building construction and electric car production to craft villages and landscape projects.

L+CC,
Ningde Village renovation project, Ningde,
2017

The architecture and landscape project is about renovating two existing villages, and designing programmes and spaces to encourage the villagers to remain in this rural region of China. Digital infrastructure for data harvesting is installed in the agriculture fields, before any architecture or landscape intervention takes place.

Technological development was one of the main pillars of the 'model city' that enabled the Chinese metropolis of Shenzhen to become the factory of the world. Different technologies were brought in to build the manufacturing spaces, the physical and online infrastructures of commerce and transportation, and the border management mechanisms around the Special Economic Zones; meanwhile the exceptional legal conditions relating to taxes, customs, labour organisation and other matters made it possible for it to be governed on its own.

Obviously, this rapid and large-scale investment in technology and urbanisation in the region has meant an ease of accessibility to technology for its citizens. Today, a smartphone with several applications and mobile internet is extremely affordable in China. Online platforms like Alibaba create easily manageable e-commerce and distribution infrastructures in economies of scale. Supply-chain management companies make production cycles more efficient. Technological transformation in modern China is not a recent phenomenon;[1] however, its acceleration with the state-controlled capitalist system in the last 30 years has made this period remarkable, and has caused a significant transformation of nature, culture and daily life. Whether in the urban sphere, or that of economy or ecology, the initiatives, individuals, makers and innovators are all part of this new 'technological order'. Aformal Academy's interest lies in researching the technologies employed in these spheres, exploring how the fringes of urban, rural, economy and technology together set the context for the transformation towards the 'post-human', as well as being influenced by it.

Hacker Robot Labs

The Pearl River Delta (PRD) region is no longer defined by the geography of delta, but spreading to other territories. For instance, the City of Huizhou, which is not essentially a part of PRD, is rapidly being linked to the region through numerous new mass-transit connections planned between Shenzhen and Huizhou. The impact of this on the city is at its periphery, where new urban development is taking place and informal tech-spaces are cropping up. Among these is a robot maker's workshop/laboratory, where the inventor/owner and his team have occupied a few apartments in a failed residential development. They experiment with machines and toys readily available on the market, mixed with high-end software, inventing new robots or producing slightly different ones. An example is the hospitality robot, similar to the ancient Chinese automaton in principle, that greets guests at the entrance to their workshop. Another one is a battle robot toy for a gaming company. The most recent example of their production is a robot currently used for simple communication with people at the immigration section on Shenzhen border checkpoints.

The phenomenon of urban periphery maker spaces is similar in Chongqing. There, caves dating back to 1000 BC, which were the first human settlements in the area and were used as shelters during the Second World War, are currently occupied by makers/hackers, bitcoin companies, small-scale production and craft shops. Being invested as one of the hubs of the Chinese government's Belt and Road Initiative – a strategy widely described as a 21st-century Silk Road – the city expects to have a more prominent position in the global trade and technology network, and does not consider this scale of production and the caves as part of that agenda, planning to clear them away. In the cases of Huizhou and Chongqing, the idea of the fringes of technology includes both the technological and the urban spheres, the marginal spaces of the city and the online space, and the ideology of invention. Machine landscapes are not necessarily all perfectly sterile spaces; they still reflect the complexity of human culture and the production process in their architecture.

Yang Xiong,
Hacker Robot Lab,
Huizhou,
2017

above: Inside the hacker space, a female hospitality robot greets the visitor at the entrance to the workshop.

right: View of the hacker space from the outside, the abandoned real-estate development site at the edge of the city. Three dismantled catering robots can be seen in front of the workshop.

Battery Factories

A factory in Zhuhai produces batteries and engines for electric car companies, enabling the production of affordable lower-speed electric cars. The factory's main market is still China; however, distributors from different countries – especially in Africa – have been buying products and vehicles from their network recently, often subsidised by the Chinese government. The motivations of the distributors are about reducing oil dependency, solving the transportation issue resulting from the lack of public transport infrastructure, and creating alternatives for/within the individual car ownership in their own countries. Meanwhile, the technology company Baidu are working on a driverless navigation technology. In this case, the fringe of technology is defined by affordable, sustainable and driverless transportation that is rapidly provided in the form of electric cars. The availability of individual cars across territories and social classes, and their aesthetic, will have a significant impact on future transportation and cities.

E-Commerce Villages

The urban transformation and increasing online presence that Dafen painters' village is going through is an echo of Shenzhen's rapid economic and urban development, as well as its new agenda to become a creative city. The rising real-estate prices, the art market intervening heavily in the urban village, and the different government policies in the last decade have made it impossible for some of the migrant painters to stay in Dafen/Shenzhen. When it was the 'factory' of the art world, producing 60 per cent of the world's paintings, this urban village was at the fringes of the city and largely ignored.[2] Since the painters' collective participation in Expo 2010 Shanghai, the village has attracted further attention from the art world, which forced it to confront the village's dynamics. Due to rising rents and other factors created by a booming city, a large number of migrant artists have been moving to cheaper cities like Xiamen and Yiwu and selling their works through online platforms. The Art Industry Association of Dafen Oil Painting Village facilitates this transition in a more visible way by partnering with an online lifestyle platform, JD.com. The transformation to a shrinking village is considered to be unfortunate for Dafen. However, it could also be interpreted as the liberation of a certain style, the Dafen method, from a specified physical territory to the digital one, by the use of online platform technologies.

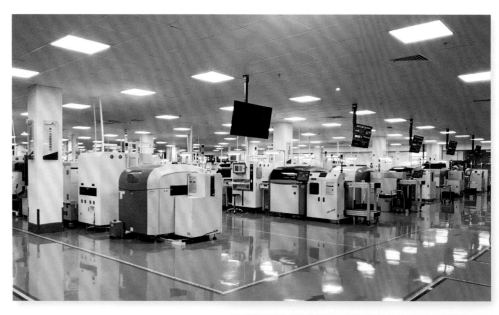

Enpower Factory,
Zhuhai,
2018

Battery production factory for electric cars.
View from the interior.

Dafen Painters' Village,
Shenzhen,
2006

An artist produces a repetition of
paintings at once, in a workshop
in the alleyways of Dafen Village.

Supply Chain Infrastructures

A similar phenomenon is occurring in Foshan, in the realm of architecture. Supply-chain management companies for building materials and components link individual clients looking to build a single house, hotel or any other typology in any location in the world to craftspeople, artists, small-scale maintenance businesses and construction-related factories in the PRD region. All the elements necessary for the architectural design to be built can be collected through an artificial-intelligence-based platform, packaged into a container, and shipped to the designated building location. This way the supply-chain managers facilitate a decentralised global crafts, design and construction infrastructure. The examples of Dafen and Foshan both show how physical space works as the infrastructure of the network, as the literal extension of the websites, where the mouse ends up as it trails off the fringe of the screen.

Ecology and Technology

Foshan hints at the production and supply-chain spaces of the PRD region, while Dafen demonstrates its extension to the countryside. The common catch-all term for these rural supply-chain extensions is 'Taobao villages', where entire villages have become de facto factories by leveraging their craft skills, global shipping and e-commerce realities.[3] Meanwhile, outside the city of Ningde, in Fujian province, contemporary technologies are implemented on fields without human presence. A company implements high-end aerial imaging technology and geographic information systems (GIS), using over 80 satellites and drones over fields and greenhouses to develop a series of 'data collection test fields' located along the valley. New factories for building the machines that will do 'data farming and harvesting' are slated for construction. From the initial phases of such development, these landscapes are strictly to be seen from above with high-end technology, whether inhabited by humans or different kinds of non-humans.

Entangled Landscapes of the Post-Human

In factories, machines physically replace human labour. In e-commerce villages, the villages are the physical extension of the online activity of humans, while the machines act as facilitators. The workshop, laboratory and factory work together with the (intelligent) online supply-chain infrastructures to reach efficiently across territories. Physical landscapes are translated to the digital with the primary aim of data harvesting, where the reason and the cause of such interventions become increasingly complex to comprehend. In other cases, such as the robot laboratory or the caves, the local initiatives differentiate from the global, appropriate, dismantle and redefine them. The local systems and infrastructures become not an isolated alternative to their global counterparts, but the latter's foil that resist being reproduced by them.

The increasing influence of technology on the transformation of urban, natural, human and (post-)human landscapes is changing culture and daily life, but also the realm of life itself. This text has presented glimpses of this transformation. The accelerating entanglement between the human and the nonhuman requires ontological approaches that go beyond an understanding of subject and object. ⌀

Notes
1. Yuk Hui, *The Question Concerning Technology in China*, Urbanomic (Falmouth), 2016.
2. Frances Arnold, 'The World's Art Factory is in Jeopardy', 22 June 2017: www.artsy.net/article/artsy-editorial-village-60-worlds-paintings-future-jeopardy.
3. Stephan Petermann, 'Put Down the Hoe, Pick Up the Mouse', 2017: www.e-flux.com/architecture/urban-village/169786/put-down-the-hoe-pick-up-the-mouse/.

Cheng Huaibao,
Bunk Bed Factory,
Taobao village in Xuzhou,
2017

A worker wielding a screeching hand-held wood sander toils overtime, to prepare for the wave of orders to come on 11 November – e-shopping day.

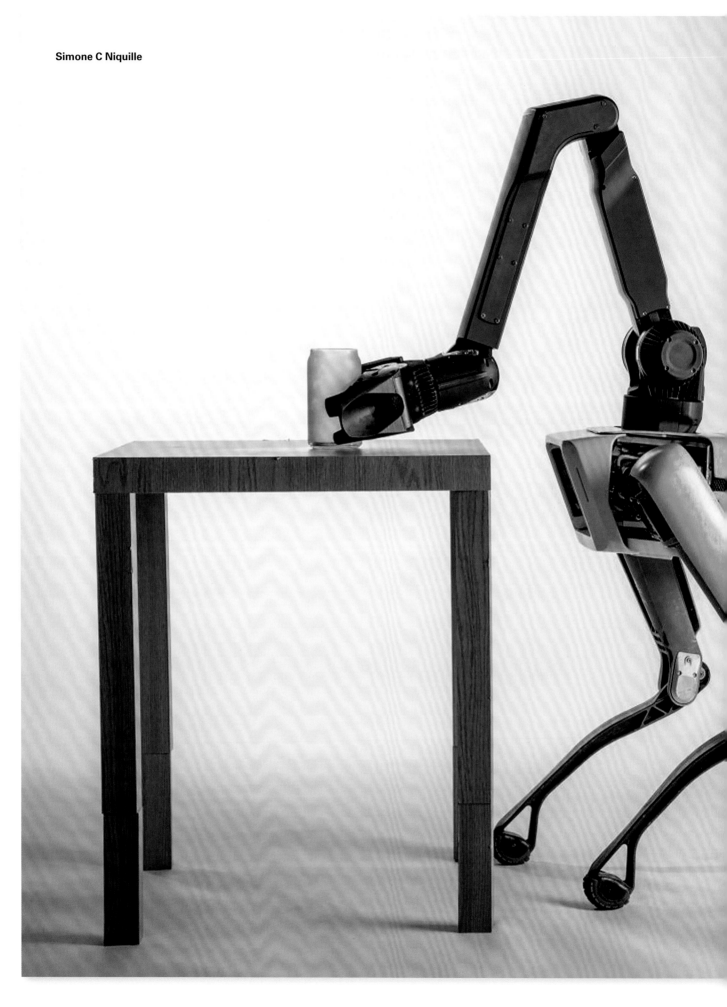

REGARDING THE PAIN OF SPOTMINI

OR WHAT A ROBOT'S STRUGGLE TO LEARN REVEALS ABOUT THE BUILT ENVIRONMENT

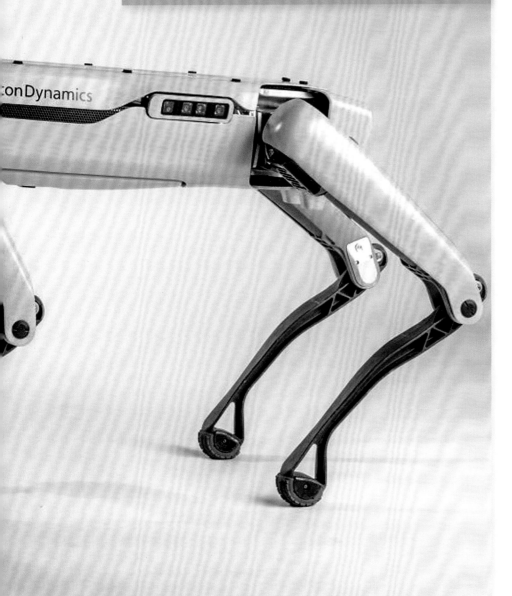

Boston Dynamics,
SpotMini,
2018

A caption generated with Microsoft's
CaptionBot, built with the company's
Computer Vision API to extract
information from images, describes
this image of the quadruped robot
SpotMini grasping a can as: 'I am not
really confident, but I think it's a black
and yellow bicycle.' SpotMini has a
height of 0.84 m (2 ft 9 in), a total of
17 joints and weighs 30 kg (66 lb). In
this image the table's legs have been
elongated to fit the robot's ergonomy.

It can feel surprisingly voyeuristic to watch a robot being put through its paces. SpotMini is a quadruped robot developed by Massachusetts firm Boston Dynamics for the commercial market and promoted through online videos. The constant fluctuation of domestic and office environments in terms of both content and configuration presents a real challenge for the computer vision that SpotMini relies on for navigation. **Simone C Niquille** – principal of Amsterdam avatar creation and identity strategy practice Technoflesh – reports on the project, exploring how such machines' parameters are defined and what the consequences are for architecture.

Boston Dynamics has been creating four-legged and biped robots since 1992, continuing the research pursued by the company's founder and CEO Marc Raibert at the MIT Leg Laboratory.[1] The research and development is primarily geared towards a defence and industry market, with its robots partaking in the DARPA (Defense Advanced Research Projects Agency) Robotics Challenge or being engineered to proxy the carry-load of soldiers. Public communication of this work largely occurs through Boston Dynamics' YouTube account. New machinic creatures boast their abilities in short clips: the videos strike a peculiar tone between slapstick comedy, meme-worthy content and engineering test footage. For example, a video titled 'Atlas, the Next Generation'[2] depicts the company's humanoid robot walking in the woods, attempting to pick up a box, leaving through a door. These videos leave the robot's intended applications obscured while the low-production recording quality renders the sophisticated technology on display mere entertainment. Seeing a robot fail is amusing, yet carries an uncanny undertone: as Susan Sontag writes in her 2003 book on photography, *Regarding the Pain of Others*, which inspired this essay's title, images are first filtered through image-takers.[3] Or in this case, autonomous robots' computer vision is first filtered through their makers. An autonomous robot's struggle to navigate spaces designed for humans reveals the designer's assumptions regarding the intended user (and the robot's failure at imitating them). Once functioning flawlessly, these assumptions causing violent consequence not only for the robot but, more importantly, for the excluded user are hermetically sealed within automation.

INTRODUCING SPOTMINI

The ambiguity of context shifts when introducing the robot SpotMini for the commercial market, a first for Boston Dynamics, with a decidedly specific scenography. 'Introducing SpotMini' (2016)[4] is filmed in a domestic environment: a house complete with living room, kitchen and dining room. Marc Raibert disclosed that the robot's development was particularly influenced by their time as a Google-owned company: 'The SpotMini robot is one that was motivated by thinking about what could go in an office – in a space more accessible for business applications – and then, the home eventually.'[5] SpotMini is the company's first robot to inhabit an environment built by and for the human body. Analysing the video's scenography thus might reveal standards of human-centred design.

The video opens at Boston Dynamics' headquarters in Waltham, Massachusetts. SpotMini is parked against a wall, neatly lined up together with the company's other creations. The video cuts to inside a vast warehouse. On the left is a pale-blue-and-white-painted facade of what looks like a suburban prefab home out of a Sears catalogue, complete with front porch but without a second floor or a roof. A fiducial marker is fixed to the porch's rail. The video shows SpotMini entering the house. The white interior walls are covered with black bump and scratch marks – evidence of the robot's training sessions. SpotMini turns around the corner into a dining room where two men are sitting at a table with empty plates and glasses. The setting resembles a film set, except that it is not.

Simone C Niquille,
Dining Room,
'Reconstructing the Boston Dynamics Test House',
2018

A rendering from underneath the dining-room table simulating SpotMini's perspective.

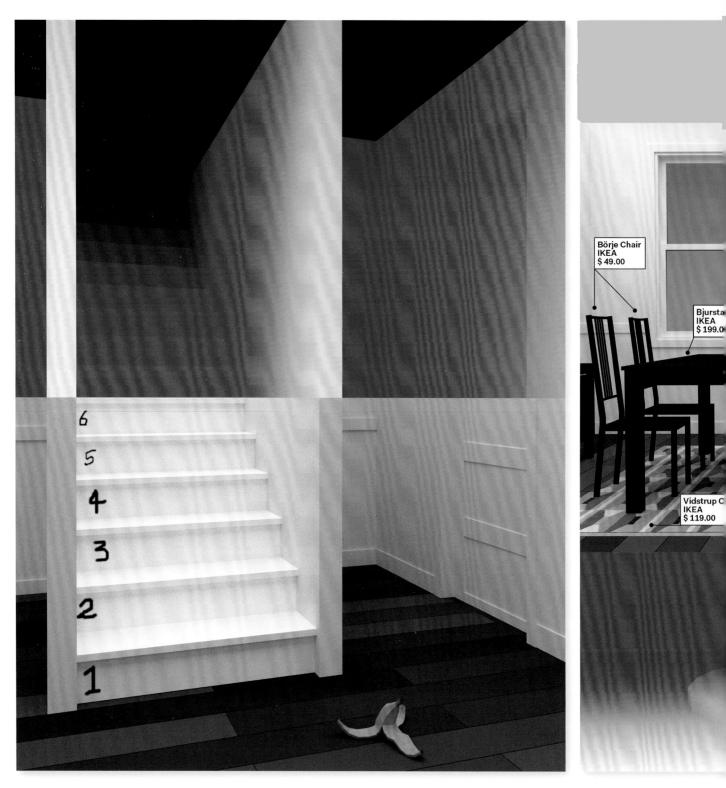

Simone C Niquille,
Stairs & Banana,
'Reconstructing the Boston Dynamics Test House',
2018

In the video 'Introducing SpotMini' the robot slips on bananas
purposely placed to showcase its ability to get back up without
assistance. The stairs, leading to a non-existent second floor,
are numbered on the riser for performance evaluation.

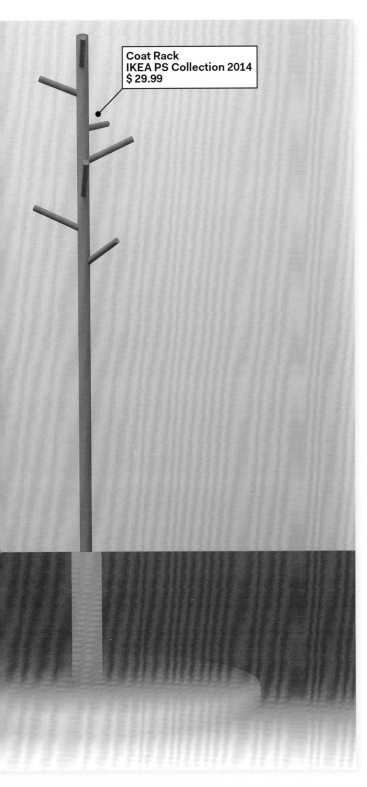

Coat Rack
IKEA PS Collection 2014
$ 29.99

To navigate and recognise objects, SpotMini relies on computer vision. More than merely illustrating a prospective client environment, the house functions as a test subject to verify SpotMini's computer vision. Like how a colour test card in photography is used to calibrate and verify 'true' representation of pigments,[6] the Boston Dynamics 'test house' evaluates object recognition and spatial orientation.

Throughout the video SpotMini is seen manoeuvring through a living room, doing the dishes and bringing a beverage to a man sitting on the couch reading Olivier Faugeras's influential 1993 book *Three-Dimensional Computer Vision*.[7] Presumably this space was not built by an architect or furnished by an interior designer but has instead been assembled by the company's engineers. Rather than comfort, the aim was an environment detailed yet unspecific enough to stand in for a range of SpotMini's future 'homes'.

The majority of identifiable items in the house are IKEA products. One particularly stands out among the otherwise mundane furnishing choices: the coat rack from IKEA's 2014 PS collection, advertised specifically for 'the fiercely independent. For free-thinkers who refuse a work-eat-sleep-repeat life and who give convention a wedgie. Not asking for permission or approval. Choosing freedom and the possibilities that come with it'[8] – a mantra descriptive of a Google office campus's synthesis of domestic and work space maximising productivity through comfort. In contrast to an Amazon fulfilment centre, designed specifically for human–machine collaboration through a strict choreography and floor plan, a domestic environment or workplace is in permanent transition. Furniture configurations are modified, groceries added, trash discarded, the amount of people in a space varied at any given time. As such, these environments are a particular challenge for computer-vision systems, which are reliant on trained standards and a degree of consistency to function.

Simone C Niquille,
IKEA PS Collection 2014 Coat Rack,
'Reconstructing the Boston Dynamics Test House',
2018

The coat rack from IKEA's PS Collection 2014 stands out as a peculiar furnishing choice in the otherwise mundane interior.

These environments are a particular challenge for computer-vision systems, which are reliant on trained standards and a degree of consistency to function.

There are only a few fiducial markers placed in the Boston Dynamics test house. Most furniture, kitchen items, floors and walls are markerless – meaning that SpotMini recognises the A&W Root Beer can on the kitchen counter as an object and does not identify it via a tagged marker. A dining-room chair might not always be located in the exact same spot but needs to be recognised and interacted with properly regardless. Therefore, certain ground truths about objects and spaces need to be established. In the Boston Dynamics test house IKEA products define furniture fundamentals. What is not visible from the test house, however, is SpotMini's classification spectrum. What parameters must an object fulfil to be classified as a chair, and at what point does it transcend the category? If a chair is defined as a four-legged raised platform with a backrest, like the Börje IKEA chair proposes, how would SpotMini's computer-vision system categorise an ergonomic kneeling chair or a Japanese zaisu? Does an increase of cohabitation between humans and autonomous machines, such as the popular Roomba vacuum cleaner, limit or even exclude variety as a result of computer vision's dependence on consistency? In 2015 a story about a Roomba 'eating the hair of a South Korean woman' sleeping on the floor of her apartment appeared in the news. The narrative was formulated as a dystopian 'man vs machine' scenario when what should have been questioned are the robot's navigational parameters, evidently not trained for the event of someone sleeping on the floor.[9] The incident thus occurred by design, not by accident.

Autonomous machines' computer-vision capabilities depend on the resolution of their training database. The database, however, is a subjective collection created by engineers, technicians or academic researchers. Once filtered through computer vision, this subjectivity becomes obscured: the seeing technology is too easily mistaken as an impartial agent. The Boston Dynamics test house is an indicator of this otherwise invisible training data. It is by no means a complete picture of the training database but points towards possible benchmarks.

SYNTHETICALLY RECONSTRUCTING THE BOSTON DYNAMICS TEST HOUSE

As an attempt to decode the construction process, the Boston Dynamics test house was synthetically reconstructed in the 3D software Blender. Most objects in the scene are not modelled but modified meshes downloaded from the SketchUp 3D Warehouse, an online repository of user-generated models geared towards architectural design 'for everyone'.[10] The inventory of the SketchUp 3D Warehouse is an indicator of the objects in demand to model architecture yet to be built. IKEA furniture's physical omnipresence translates to the virtual.

Because of the large amount of freely available models in online libraries such as the SketchUp 3D Warehouse, these repositories are scraped by researchers to create synthetic test databases for computer-vision and image-recognition algorithms. Synthetic images are used in the development of such algorithms to establish a ground truth. Using synthetically constructed objects and scenes is more efficient in establishing a ground truth than by images that first have to be annotated through human labour. One such database is the MIT 'Dataset for IKEA 3D models and aligned images'[11] from 2013 which is used to train an image-recognition algorithm to recognise furniture in photographs and align their position in three-dimensional space with a matching 3D model. Such training datasets rely on large amounts of data. Because of its ubiquity, IKEA furniture is ideal: the SketchUp library contains 3D models while photography sites such as Flickr can be mined for furniture photographs. The Princeton Shape Benchmark[12] from 2005 is another such example that made use of the SketchUp library. It attempted to 'promote the use of standardised data sets and evaluation methods for research in matching, classification, clustering, and recognition of 3D models'.[13] If successful, the Princeton Shape Benchmark would ultimately function as a standard training dataset and as such homogenise and inform all technology trained by it. Computer vision's demand for standards excludes as a result all that is not contained in these databases.

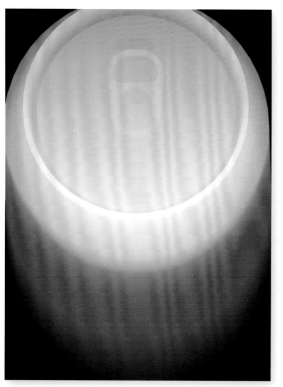

Simone C Niquille,
A&W Root Beer Can,
'Reconstructing the Boston Dynamics Test House',
2018

left: A depth-map image of a beverage can. In the video 'Introducing SpotMini' the robot recognises a can as an object, without the proxy of a fiducial marker.

Simone C Niquille,
Boston Dynamics Test House,
'Reconstructing the Boston Dynamics Test House',
2018

opposite: A floor plan of the SpotMini test facility rendered as a depth map representing distance from the camera's viewpoint with a receding gradient.

TESTING ROBUSTNESS

In the video 'Testing Robustness' (2018),[14] the four-legged robot SpotMini is seen attempting to open a door and walk through it (or escape, depending on one's interpretation of the narrative) while a person wearing protective glasses is violently disrupting the robot's attempts with a hockey stick. Intended as a durability test demonstrating the robot's abilities in navigating an environment built by and for humans, the video also reads as a depiction of wilfully inflicted pain by a 'human' on a 'non-human'. As such the video is an urgent reminder to challenge standards of who is or is not 'human', a definition too often taken for granted in design and architectural disciplines.

A note at the end of the video's description assures that 'This testing does not irritate or harm the robot.' Regardless, as viewer it is hard to shake the feeling of having witnessed an abusive display of power. The technical description of SpotMini explains that the robot is not yet fully autonomous but partially controlled via remote control. The robot, it is therefore assured, is not sentient. There is no pain. The machine simply impartially completes the input task regardless of interference.

SpotMini's physical abuse is not the only display of violence in the video. The robot's sole mission is to open and pass through a door, albeit one designed to 'human' body measurement standards and thus ergonomically inaccurate to the robot's proportions. Body standardisation is a soft power. Built into the environment by design, these standardisations define the height of handles, width, length, weight and material of doors, windows, walls, furniture and as such define who does or does not have access. In the video, the door is a literal point of passing: by successfully completing its task – opening and walking through the door – SpotMini does not become 'human', but rather reinforces the extent to which it does not fit.

GLITCHING STANDARDS

The door is an indicator of the degree to which standards define the built environment and product design. By introducing computer-vision-reliant autonomous machines as cohabitants, existing standards are prone to be absorbed while new benchmarks are established, such as is evident from the Boston Dynamics test house or the Princeton Shape Benchmark. Rather than measuring computer vision's ability to recognise by a success rate, failure to 'correctly' identify exposes the otherwise hidden. Instead of interpreting a Roomba vacuuming a woman's hair as a robot's attack on humanity, it reveals the manufacturer's assumptions of sleep patterns, furniture and culture. As such, glitches occurring during the development of seeing technologies should be used to disclose established standards, creating opportunities to evaluate rather than impose. ⌀

NOTES
1. 'MIT Leg Laboratory': www.ai.mit.edu/projects/leglab/home.html.
2. 'Atlas, the Next Generation': www.youtube.com/watch?v=rVlhMGQgDkY.
3. Susan Sontag, *Regarding the Pain of Others*, Farrar, Straus and Giroux (New York), 2003.
4. 'Introducing SpotMini': www.youtube.com/watch?v=tf7IEVTDjng.
5. 'Marc Raibert at the Tech Crunch Sessions 2018': www.youtube.com/watch?v=QIJ_-iVbah8.
6. Lorna Roth, 'Looking at Shirley, the Ultimate Norm: Colour Balance, Image Technologies, and Cognitive Equity', *Canadian Journal of Communication*, 34 (1), 2009, pp 111–36.
7. Olivier Faugeras, *Three-Dimensional Computer Vision: A Geometric Viewpoint*, MIT Press (Cambridge, MA), 1993.
8. 'IKEA PS Collection': www.IKEA.com/us/en/catalog/categories/collections/12041.
9. Justin McCurry, 'South Korean Woman's Hair Eaten by Robot Vacuum Cleaner', *The Guardian*, 9 February 2015: www.theguardian.com/world/2015/feb/09/south-korean-womans-hair-eaten-by-robot-vacuum-cleaner-as-she-slept.
10. 'SketchUp 3D Warehouse': www.sketchup.com.
11. 'Dataset for IKEA 3D models and aligned images': http://IKEA.csail.mit.edu.
12. 'Princeton Shape Benchmark': http://shape.cs.princeton.edu/benchmark.
13. *Ibid*.
14. 'Testing Robustness': www.youtube.com/watch?v=aFuA50H9uek.

By successfully completing its task – opening and walking through the door – SpotMini does not become 'human', but rather reinforces the extent to which it does not fit.

Tim Maughan

No One Driv

Autonomous Vehicles
But is Anyone Taking

Futuristic Detroit as seen through the
LIDAR scanner machine vision of self-
driving cars in Young's and Maughan's
short film *Where the City Can't See*.

ne's
ing

Will Reshape Cities,
Control of How?

Driverless cars promise to be a seductive, inevitable technology that will transform our cities in a multitude of ways. But, asks author and journalist **Tim Maughan**, are we really prepared for what lies ahead, or have we already fallen asleep at the wheel?

As I sit down to write this in May 2018, news is breaking of another accident involving a self-driving car. A Tesla Model S, which the driver claims was in Autopilot, has crashed into a parked police car in Laguna Beach, California.[1] Autopilot is what Tesla calls its semi-autonomous driving mode, which the company likes to refer to as a kind of advanced cruise-control. In a press statement following the accident the company repeated its increasingly familiar refrain that 'Tesla has always been clear that Autopilot doesn't make the car impervious to all accidents'.[2] Earlier the same month, the US National Highway Traffic Safety Administration (NHTSA) sent a team to investigate the crash of a Tesla vehicle in South Jordan, Utah, that smashed into a fire truck stopped at a red light. Police reports say data from the car showed that Autopilot was enabled less than 90 seconds before the crash.[3] The agency is also investigating a crash in January last year where a Tesla in Autopilot struck – again – a parked fire truck.[4]

Nobody died in any of these incidents, luckily. But the NHTSA is also investigating a fatal crash in March that involved a Tesla Model X using Autopilot that struck a highway divider in Mountain View, California.[5] It was, at the time of writing, the fourth fatality in an autonomous car, and the third in a Tesla.[6] It is incredibly bad timing for boy-wonder Elon Musk's car company, as the auto manufacturer faces increasing rumours and reports questioning its financial viability. It has struggled to bring down prices and maintain a strong market share while watching the innovations it built its reputation on – electric power and advanced high-tech features such as Autopilot – become standard on the cars of its much larger, more mainstream and established competitors. The last thing it needs is the suggestion that its vehicles might be as unsafe as its production lines (a Worksafe report from 2017 showed that injury rates at Tesla's Fremont plant were 31 per cent higher than the national industry average, with ambulances being called to the factory over 100 times in three years).[7]

James Bridle,
Autonomous Trap 001,
Mount Parnassus,
central Greece,
2017

By quickly deploying road markings
– in the form of a salt circle – James
Bridle confuses the self-driving
car's vision system into believing
it is surrounded by no-entry points.

Autonomous Safety: Too Early to Tell

Claims from self-driving evangelists and Musk's vocal army of fans on social media that the technology is still in its very early days and promises to be far safer than human drivers in the long run have some potential validity. The problem is it is just far too early to tell if that is the case. One of the key industry metrics for comparing the safety levels for autonomous cars versus human drivers is the number of fatalities per 100 million miles driven. Currently humans are involved in approximately 1.8 fatalities, but when it comes to autonomous vehicles we are nowhere near having that amount of data yet; in order to make realistic comparisons they would have to be driven hundreds of millions more miles in full autonomous mode. As of February 2018, autonomous vehicles from Google's Waymo have covered a mere 5 million miles,[8] and all of them with a human driver who monitors and takes control when needed – which was, on average, necessary every 5,600 miles. According to the *New York Times*, in Uber's self-driving research programme this was as low as just 13 miles.[9]

But the real elephant in the room when discussing Tesla, self-driving cars and safety records is regulation, or the lack thereof. Both Google and Uber's research programmes involve cars operating in public spaces and amongst human traffic, but both have been carried out in partnership with city authorities. When an autonomous Uber killed a pedestrian in March 2018 its programme – in partnership with the city of Tempe, Arizona – was immediately suspended by both the company and the city authority.[10] But Tesla has never tested its technology in such a formal way – Autopilot was offered as a software upgrade to existing Tesla owners, with Musk himself describing it as 'the same as updating your phone or your laptop … A huge part of what Tesla is, is a Silicon Valley software company.'[11] As such, instead of working with regulators, city authorities and safety agencies, Tesla's approach has been to dump their code into an existing market and let users beta test it themselves. While that is an understandable, if often infuriating, approach when it comes to smartphone apps or video games, it is not hard to see how it can be a potentially fatal model for high-end cars on public roads.

Where Does the Buck Stop?

It also exposes one of the biggest legal issues surrounding autonomous vehicles: who is responsible when they go wrong? If the owner of the vehicle is not in control at the time an accident happens, then are they legally responsible? If not them, then who? The manufacturer? The software engineer that wrote the code? The car itself? It is an obviously huge question that threatens to spawn a whole subdiscipline of ethics around itself, and while Silicon Valley tech evangelists insist the blockchain will somehow solve everything, there is an obvious point where it stops being a philosophical or technological problem and becomes one that needs the legal system, regulators and governments to step in and make a decision. There is little indication that we are close to reaching that point yet.

If driverless cars crashing themselves was not bad enough, then there is the worry that they can be interfered with. If self-driving cars are basically just large, complex, networked computers on wheels then they are also vulnerable to the same kinds of hacks, security breaches and electronic assaults as any computer system. In 2017 artist James Bridle grabbed headlines with his Autonomous Car Trap project, which uses staged photos to show how self-driving cars might be confused just by drawing white lines around them.[12] An intriguing speculative project that draws as much on tech-hipsters' current obsession with magic and the occult as it does from automation anxiety, it is a powerful visual reminder of how easily technology can be duped and subverted by human ingenuity.

The salt circle is a traditional form of protection in magical practice. Artist James Bridle uses one to confuse a self-driving car.

Liam Young and Tim Maughan,
Where the City Can't See,
Detroit,
2016

Futuristic Detroit as seen through the LIDAR scanner
machine vision of self-driving cars in Young's
and Maughan's short film *Where the City Can't See*.

In 2016 Liam Young and myself made *Where the City Can't See*, a short film shot entirely with LIDAR scanners, the laser-based vision system used by Google's and Uber's self-driving cars. Set in a futuristic Detroit that has become a heavily surveilled and highly automated factory for self-driving cars, it tells the story of teenagers organising illegal parties while hiding themselves – and even whole buildings – by wearing clothes made from 'deflection fabrics'. These materials, the patterns of which are designed to deflect and diffuse the LIDAR's laser scans, make them invisible to the eyes of automated vehicles. The film's characters also use low bass frequencies to disrupt LIDAR, and QRcode flyers to divert automated taxi cabs into taking them to hidden, secret locations. Although again a speculative work, these hacks are based on real-world exploits of LIDAR and machine-vision systems.

A more frightening and visceral example of interference is the work of Charlie Miller and Chris Valasek (a security researcher at Twitter, and director of vehicle security research at IOActive) hacking existing, non-autonomous cars, as detailed in Andy Greenberg's article for *Wired* [13] back in 2015, where they were able to hijack his Jeep Cherokee's air conditioning, stereo, displays, windscreen wipers and even brakes while Greenberg was driving it at 70 miles per hour (113 kilometres per hour) on the highway. The report led to Jeep and other manufacturers updating their security procedures, but it is a terrifying example of how cars have already become complex digital systems that are just as vulnerable to hackers as our computers or smartphones.

Set in a futuristic Detroit that has become a heavily surveilled and highly automated factory for self-driving cars, it tells the story of teenagers organising illegal parties while hiding themselves – and even whole buildings – by wearing clothes made from 'deflection fabrics'.

Liam Young and Tim Maughan,
Where the City Can't See,
Detroit,
2016

above top: Partygoers wear clothes made from laser-reflecting fabrics
to distort and confuse the machine-vision systems of self-driving cars.

above: As the Detroit of *Where the City Can't See* becomes dominated
by machines and self-driving cars, the last factory workers repurpose
the abandoned human-scale spaces for illegal raves.

It seems like autonomous,
self-driving vehicles are
inevitable, and beyond
the futuristic luxury
that excites us they will
provide real convenience
and benefits to many.

A Nation of Truck Drivers

There are, however, much larger issues appearing on the horizon. In 2015 National Public Radio (NPR) published a map of the US which showed the most popular occupation in each state, based on statistics from the US Census Bureau.[14] In all but 16 states it was 'truck driver'. An estimated 1.7 million Americans make a living from driving trucks. While most of the popular public attention has focused on self-driving personal cars, there is an obvious push to develop autonomous trucks, with companies such as Tesla and Volvo close to bringing vehicles to market. It is hard to imagine what the impact could be, almost overnight, to one of the planet's most popular professions.

Except we do not have to imagine too hard. One job has already been critically wounded by technological disruption: driving a taxi or cab, and so far the picture is bleak. As the *New York Times* reported in May 2018, at least five New York City cab drivers have committed suicide this year as a result of Uber's much-lauded 'disruption'.[15] The city's medallion permit system, which was meant to limit the number of cab drivers, has become meaningless in the face of unregulated competition. Uber, Lyft and other ride-sharing platforms have ripped apart what was once a stable and in-demand job, usually associated with blue-collar workers and immigrant populations, and made it just as precarious as the gig economy jobs that are replacing it. If and when autonomous cars come to market it is hard to see it continuing to exist as a job at all.

The usual response from self-driving proponents is not to worry. This is just how technological change works, it alters society. What happened to all the horse-drawn carriage jobs, they say, when the car was introduced? The same technological breakthroughs will create new jobs. Everyone just needs to learn to code. It is a short-term problem, they say, that will be for the best in the long term.

The problem is we do not, for the most part, live in a society that values long-term planning. We live in a society where decisions are made by market forces, not by experts, forecasters or economic planners. We live in a society where, as shown by Trump and Brexit, increasingly the voting population reacts to perceived threats to their livelihood by electing dangerously incompetent leaders or making irreversibly catastrophic choices about the future of their nation. And we live in cities where the same market forces, in the form of property speculation and overdevelopment, have hollowed out our central urban environments of working-class and immigrant populations, and where this migration of labour is being solved not by planning and building affordable housing, but by automation – whether that is in the form of McDonald's self-service kiosks, Amazon's prototype staffless grocery stores, or yes, Uber and Google's self-driving taxi projects.

It seems like autonomous, self-driving vehicles are inevitable, and beyond the futuristic luxury that excites us they will provide real convenience and benefits to many. But without clear regulation, leadership and a willingness to predict and plan for the changes they will bring they threaten to wreak havoc among certain populations, and to further reduce the diversity and potential of our increasingly clinical and gentrified cities. Now, before it is too late, we need to take the wheel, and take control. ⌁

Notes

1. David Grossman, 'Tesla Hits Cop Car While Allegedly on Autopilot', *Popular Mechanics*, 30 May 2018: www.popularmechanics.com/cars/car-technology/a20963081/tesla-hits-cop-car-while-allegedly-on-autopilot/.
2. David Shepardson, 'Tesla Hits Parked California Police Vehicle; Driver Blames 'Autopilot', Reuters.com, 29 May 2018: www.reuters.com/article/us-tesla-autopilot/tesla-hits-parked-california-police-vehicle-driver-blames-autopilot-idUSKCN1IU2SZ.
3. *Ibid.*
4. David Grossman, 'Tesla Crashes Into Fire Truck While Reportedly on Autopilot', *Popular Mechanics*, 23 January 2018: www.popularmechanics.com/cars/hybrid-electric/a15855035/tesla-crashes-into-fire-truck-while-reportedly-on-autopilot/.
5. 'Tesla Car that Crashed and Killed Driver was Running on Autopilot, Firm Says', *The Guardian*, 31 March 2018: www.theguardian.com/technology/2018/mar/31/tesla-car-crash-autopilot-mountain-view.
6. Shepardson, *op cit.*
7. Worksafe, 'Analysis of Tesla Injury Rates: 2014 to 2017', 24 May 2017: https://worksafe.typepad.com/files/worksafe_tesla5_24.pdf.
8. 'Waymo Reaches 5 Million Self-driven Miles', *Medium*, 27 February 2018: https://medium.com/waymo/waymo-reaches-5-million-self-driven-miles-61fba590fafe.
9. Daisuke Wakabayashi, 'Uber's Self-driving Cars were Struggling Before Arizona Crash', *New York Times*, 23 March 2018: www.nytimes.com/2018/03/23/technology/uber-self-driving-cars-arizona.html
10. Julia Belluz, 'A Self-driving Uber Car Killed a Pedestrian. Human Drivers will Kill 16 People Today', *Vox*, 19 March 2018: www.vox.com/science-and-health/2018/3/19/17139868/self-driving-uber-killed-pedestrian-human-drivers-deadly.
11. 'Elon Musk: Model S Not a Car but a "Sophisticated Computer on Wheels"', *LA Times*, 19 March 2015: www.latimes.com/business/autos/la-fi-hy-musk-computer-on-wheels-20150319-story.html.
12. Beckett Mufson, 'Meet the Artist Using Ritual Magic to Trap Self-Driving Cars', *Vice*, 18 March 2017: www.vice.com/en_us/article/ywwba5/meet-the-artist-using-ritual-magic-to-trap-self-driving-cars.
13. 'Hackers Remotely Kill a Jeep on the Highway – With Me in It', *Wired*, 21 July 2016: www.wired.com/2015/07/hackers-remotely-kill-jeep-highway/.
14. 'Map: The Most Common* Job In Every State', National Public Radio, 5 February 2015: www.npr.org/sections/money/2015/02/05/382664837/map-the-most-common-job-in-every-state.
15. Nikita Stewart and Luis Ferré-Sadurní, 'Another Taxi Driver in Debt Takes His Life: That's 5 in 5 Months', *New York Times*, 27 May 2018: www.nytimes.com/2018/05/27/nyregion/taxi-driver-suicide-nyc.html.

But without clear regulation, leadership and a willingness to predict and plan for the changes they will bring they threaten to wreak havoc.

Text © 2019 John Wiley & Sons Ltd. Images: pp 92–3, 96–8 © Liam Young; pp 94–5 © James Bridle 2017. Courtesy of the artist

Disciplinary Hybrids

Clare Lyster

Retail Landscapes of the Post-Human City

What does the rise of automated retail mean for our future? Architect **Clare Lyster**, who is Associate Professor at the University of Illinois at Chicago, looks at its various emerging forms: cashierless grocery stores, low-cost solar-powered mobile retail units, self-driving food delivery vehicles, walls of QR codes in public places … Rather than signalling a dystopian future of diminishing human interaction, she sees them as being in the lineage of work by visionary architects and urbanists from the 1960s such as Yona Friedman and Cedric Price, with the potential to increase urban equitability and empower remote communities.

Wheelys Moby Mart mobile store, Shanghai, 2017

Night-time image of the beta version of the cashierless mobile store in Shanghai. This prototype for an automated mobile store can drive itself to where it is needed as well as to a warehouse to be restocked.

Over the last 150 years, the industrial spaces of capitalist production have been the location for advancements in automation, cultivating the cyborg-worker conundrum and furthering the promise of a post-human ecosystem. Today logistics marks the latest phase of industrial automation, where sophisticated software systems and digital infrastructure render production processes and delivery schedules beyond the competencies of humans. Take, for example, how algorithms, radio-frequency identification (RFID) technology and robots choreograph the way goods are ordered, received, picked and sorted in an Amazon fulfilment centre.

However, in tandem with advances in the industrial realm, the notion of a post-human society can also be witnessed in more everyday spaces as logistical technologies burst outside the walls of the factory to render automation an increasingly quotidian phenomenon. This is legible in the range of available gadgets that have entered the home (AI home assistants to smart devices) as well as new machine-retail environments that exemplify how and where post-human landscapes are entering the public spaces of the city.

Machine Landscapes of the Everyday

Amazon opened a prototype cashierless store known as Amazon Go in Seattle in late 2017. There are no assistants and no cashiers. Customers take products from shelves that are automatically charged to their Amazon account. It is not unlike taking something from the minibar in your hotel room and having the cost appear on your bill. But worry not, Amazon promises that if you put back the item it will disappear from your balance. A combination of deep learning algorithms, sensors and cameras in the ceiling control the selection, placement and replacement of all the goods, rendering obsolete the iconic barcode, the technology that first led to automatic digital inventories in the mid-1970s. With Amazon Go's system, named 'Just Walk Out', one simply picks up an item and then leaves the store.[1] Photos of the space depict a fairly typical (if not banal) interior layout, save the entrance, which is more akin to a subway station in that turnstiles prevent entry unless you successfully scan the details of your Amazon.com account from your smartphone. With such controlled access, and surveillance, there is no browsing or loitering here.[2] Welcome to the automated city.

Amazon Go,
Seattle,
2017

The store in Seattle opened in 2017. This interior view shows the extent of sensors and information systems demanded for this type of retail.

If your phone is required to proceed deep into Amazon Go, you will need it to open the door of Moby Mart. As the name suggests, this is a mobile store that is part vehicle, part architectural space. It runs on electricity powered by solar panels and drives itself to a warehouse to restock. A drone landing platform on the roof allows merchandise to be delivered, while a hologram assistant greets customers.[3] Developed by the Swedish firm Wheelys (of Wheelys cafe-on-a-bike fame), the logic of Moby is to provide convenience, but the company also claims a political motive.[4] Moby, it is hoped, can compete with multinational corporations like Amazon, who can invest large sums of money in research and development to advance automated systems in the city (Amazon have numerous patents in the works, including a kiosk that enables one to automatically return items purchased online). According to its developers, Moby is cheap to build ($100,000) and very flexible, making it easier for laypeople to go into the retail industry. Furthermore, communities in remote locations could also purchase one to self-sustain themselves. It is currently being tested in Shanghai.

A virtual store in a train station in Seoul comprises images and codes of everyday products and groceries laminated on a wall. Installed by Tesco Homeplus in 2011, customers use their smartphones to capture QR codes of required items for home delivery.[5] By 2015, there were 22 stores in Korea.

Tesco's mobile device applications for Android, 2018

The Tesco supermarket application is used by customers for online purchases. In Seoul, South Korea, Tesco Homeplus customers use a similar app to order items from a virtual mural with images and corresponding QR codes of over 500 products.

This is a mobile store that is part vehicle, part architectural space. It runs on electricity powered by solar panels and drives itself to a warehouse to restock.

Alibaba, the Chinese online retailer, is prototyping an automated car-vending facility for Ford. One facility opened in Guangdong in March 2018. Customers select an electric car online, and pick it up at the vending centre after having been identified by facial recognition technology courtesy of a selfie uploaded by the customer at the time of placing the order. The customer has three days to try out the car before deciding to keep or return it.[6] This is not unlike a facility implemented by the online auto retailer Carvana, who opened the first car vending machine in the US in 2013, in Atlanta. And in late 2016, Autobahn Motors, a car dealership in Singapore, opened a 15-floor car-vending machine that dispenses luxury vehicles. Presumably some people never know when they might want a Ferrari!

In addition, new forms of automatic distribution are being made possible by logistical couriers from Grubhub to Yodel, many of which are now testing robots for delivery.[7] DoorDash and Postmates are working with Starship Technologies to test the robotic delivery of food in business campuses in Silicon Valley. Characterised as a cooler on wheels, these little gizmos use AI technology to navigate (they even acknowledge traffic lights). Controlled by cameras and sensors and travelling at 4 miles (6.4 kilometres) per hour, they are designed to deliver goods locally in 15 to 30 minutes within a 2-mile (3.2-kilometre) radius. They can also be seen on the streets of cities in Germany and the Netherlands, where they are being tested by Domino's Pizza;[8] while Just Eat and logistics firm Hermes are conducting trials in London and Hamburg.[9] The sidewalk is now a machine landscape. Take care when walking the dog!

Moby and its bot siblings such as Robomart, a self-driving delivery vehicle stacked with food items – akin to a vending machine on wheels that comes to you on request[10] – promise to change how retail is conducted in the city, although they are not completely original prototypes. Mobile stores called Rolling Stores were familiar in the US from 1910,[11] and many readers may remember the milkman making deliveries in his truck. Vending machines have been around since the Roman city, when machines dispensed holy water, while a book-vending machine dubbed the 'Penguincubator' was invented by Allen Lane, the founder of publishers Penguin Books, in 1937. In fact, it is worth mentioning here other early network technologies crucial to automated retail systems in the contemporary era: the credit card (1958), the ATM machine (1966) and the barcode (1974) are especially significant, not to forget the mail-order catalogue industry in the US, which at the height of its agency in the early 20th century was a predecessor of online retail.

The Machine as Disciplinary Agent

For some, that the abstract technologies currently so well rehearsed in industrial facilities would seep into the everyday to restructure the physical environment is a dystopian prospect. Nonetheless, even if some narratives – especially those centred on how automated exchange might erase collective interaction – are well founded, other declarations for machine infrastructure in contemporary urban discourse can be identified.

Tallest car vending machine in Singapore, 2017

Autobahn Motors is a 15-storey vending machine that sells luxury cars. Customers complete their purchase online via an app and the car is delivered.

Starship Technologies self-driving robotic delivery vehicle, London, 2016

Parcels and groceries are delivered from stores or hubs within a 2-mile (3.2-kilometre) radius, on request via a mobile app. It takes 15 to 30 minutes for the shipment to arrive, and the robot's journey can be tracked by the customer.

In the 1960s, architects embraced computational technologies and electronic gizmos as necessary vehicles for architectural discourse. Some focused on cybernetic theory (feedback systems) to render space more customisable. The French architect Yona Friedman invented the flatwriter, a data interface (akin to a smart typewriter) that allowed house buyers to configure their own home within a large megastructural grid that he had proposed for Paris. Others deployed networked components to conceive urbanity as distributed fields in the logic that cities would benefit by a shift from large centralised power structures to small-scale, neighbourhood-based systems that were more flexible and contingent on local needs. Cedric Price's project titled *Atom* (1962) deployed radios, televisions, calculators and screens in combination with furniture, as well as architectural space, in the design of an alternative learning platform that would render education accessible to all, especially those neglected by traditional institutional settings.[12] In a similar fashion, the technology writer James Bridle argues that Allen Lane's real genius in conceiving the Penguincubator was 'to take the book beyond the library and the traditional bookstore, into railway stations, chain stores and onto the streets'.[13]

If customisation and atomisation of institutions were the potential outcomes of urban technology in an earlier era, then today, with even smarter systems at play, the promise to rescript the city in a more equitable way is more plausible than ever. Moby, the automated food mobile, can be located in small remote sites or in areas where real estate is too expensive for services with low turnover and modest profit margins. Too often urban planning premises economies of scale, resulting in corporate dominance in the city. For example, take the downtowns of many major American cities, where development hinges on an 'anchor tenant', which is typically a big franchise with resources to invest in and occupy large floor plates. The downside here is that the corporate franchise model currently espoused by developers in cities produces banal urbanism – Paris's Champs-Élysées ends up looking the same as London's Oxford Street, while the only cultural production is consumer capitalism, in the form of cheap imports and fast fashion.

In this context, the potential for automated retail is a more diverse, cost-effective and eclectic way to think about shopping in the city and serve communities that are classified as food islands or beyond profitable delivery boundaries. Small automated retail pods are not only economically feasible but offer other bandwidths of urbanism and thus new forms of cultural production. Moreover, machine infrastructure provides a different form of retail entrepreneurship, allowing an alternative to the labour-capital that currently exists in the industrial-retail apparatus. Rather than working in a store for the minimum wage (or, worse, on commission), one can rent an automated retail pod and market one's own creative talents. In this way, the irony of automated retail infrastructure is this: while born from the logistical intelligence of industrial capitalism, it might actually deliver the opposite effect – that is, accomplish 1960s radical and anti-establishment pledges of an independent lifestyle based on self-management and a personalised relationship between work and production.

New Typologies

While machine infrastructure of the logistical era fulfils the promises that postwar computing technologies and cybernetic theories could only allude to, at the same time, making good on an old claim is not enough. To this, an additional hypothesis is offered. That automated retail is part vehicular system, part information network and part architectural interior implies that urbanity is now extended beyond architectural form to new hybrid species of space. Rather than being articulated solely by building figure, the city is, instead, composed of smart, dynamic, responsive entities developed equally across multiple design disciplines, from information to industrial and from product to graphic design. Automated landscapes thus open up the design of the city to a range of creative stakeholders and, by extension, to an array of new spatial typologies and their corresponding effects. ∆

Notes
1. Tony Peng, 'Amazon Go vs Alibaba Tao Cafe: Staffless Shop Showdown', *Medium*, 21 January 2018: https://medium.com/syncedreview/amazon-go-vs-alibaba-tao-cafe-staffless-shop-showdown-3f3929393d62.
2. Nick Wingfield, 'Inside Amazon Go, a Store of the Future', *New York Times*, 21 January 2018: www.nytimes.com/2018/01/21/technology/inside-amazon-go-a-store-of-the-future.html.
3. Adele Peters, 'The Grocery Store Of The Future Is Mobile, Self-Driving, And Run By AI', *Fast Company*, 13 June 2017: www.fastcompany.com/40429419/this-tiny-grocery-store-is-mobile-self-driving-and-run-by-ai?lipi=urn%3Ali%3Apage%3Ad_flagship3_feed%3BeE7B%2F7AoSt6iYiwcV7IANg%3D%3D.
4. Emma Tucker, 'Wheelys' Mobile Mart is a Self-Driving Store with a Holographic Shop Assistant', *Dezeen*, 28 June 2017: www.dezeen.com/2017/06/28/wheelys-self-driving-moby-mart-grocery-store-holographic-shop-assistant-design-technology/.
5. Clare Lyster, 'Logistics as Urban Choreography', *Harvard Design Magazine* 47, Winter 2017, pp 10–16.
6. Brad Jones, 'Alibaba Unveils Plans for an Electric Vehicle Vending Machine', *Futurism*, 14 December 2017: https://futurism.com/alibaba-unveils-plans-electric-vehicle-vending-machine/.
7. 'Starship Technologies Launches Pilot Program with Domino's Pizza Enterprises', *Starship*, 29 March 2017: www.starship.xyz/press_releases/starship-technologies-launches-pilot-program-with-dominos-pizza-enterprises/.
8. Malek Murison, 'Hermes and Starship Technologies to Test Delivery Robots in London', *Internet of Business*, 13 April 2017: https://internetofbusiness.com/hermes-starship-delivery-robots-london/.
9. Matt Simon, 'San Francisco Just Put The Brakes On Delivery Robots', *Wired*, 6 December 2017: www.wired.com/story/san-francisco-just-put-the-brakes-on-delivery-robots/.
10. Jonathan Schieber, 'Robomart Is The Latest Startup To Try And Unseat The Local Convenience Store', *Techcrunch*, 6 January 2018: https://techcrunch.com/2018/01/05/robomart-is-the-latest-startup-to-try-and-unseat-the-local-convenience-store/
11. Emelyn Rude, 'Like a Rolling Store: These Mobile Shops Changed Rural American Life', *Time*, 24 May 2016: http://time.com/4344621/history-rolling-store/
12. Kathy Velikov, 'Tuning Up the City: Cedric Price's Detroit Think Grid', *Journal of Architectural Education*, 69 (1), 2015, pp 40–52.
13. James Bridle, 'What Publishers Today Can Learn from Allen Lane: Fearlessness', *Publishing Perspectives*, 28 April 2010: https://publishingperspectives.com/2010/04/what-publishers-today-can-learn-from-allen-lane-fearlessness/

GHOST IN THE MACHINE

SPACE JUNK AND THE FUTURE OF EARTH ORBIT

Alice Gorman

TS
HE
INE

Van Allen probes,
2012

The probes study the harsh electromagnetic
conditions in the Van Allen belts that sit
somewhere between 1,000 and 6,000
kilometres (620 and 3,730 miles) above the
Earth. Usually satellites avoid this area as the
highly charged particles can damage them.

Hundreds of millions of objects are orbiting our planet, 94 per cent of
which are pure machine debris. Space archaeologist **Alice Gorman**, who is
Senior Lecturer at Flinders University in Adelaide, Australia, takes this *D*'s
investigations beyond the Earth's surface and out into the near universe
– looking at the material and cultural implications of the status quo, and
reflecting on possibilities for the years and centuries to come.

In the 60 years since the launch of Sputnik 1 in 1957, over 23,000 human-made objects larger than 10 centimetres (4 inches), and more than 100 million smaller fragments, have accumulated between Low Earth Orbit and the so-called 'graveyard orbit', between approximately 200 and 40,000 kilometres (125 and 24,855 miles) above the surface of the Earth.[1] A mere 6 per cent of these objects are operational spacecraft. Their chronological range is from 1958 (Vanguard 1, the oldest surviving spacecraft) until the present time. In weight, the accumulated debris is estimated to be 6,000 tons. This 'space junk' represents far more than just a hazard to operating satellites – as it is regarded by the space industry – or an all-too-familiar pollution problem. It is the repository of human ideologies and values – capitalist, communist, mercantile, colonial, gendered, scientific, environmental and cosmological.

Satellites go beyond the limits of human bodies to be our senses in the void. With the exception of a few space stations, Earth orbit has become a robotic frontier. These high-velocity orbiting machines are barely visible from Earth. They are separated from us in space and time, remotely controlled, yet highly autonomous.[2] After launch, it is the rare spacecraft that returns intact. If they draw too close to the Earth in their perpetual fall, for their hubris they are consumed in fire.

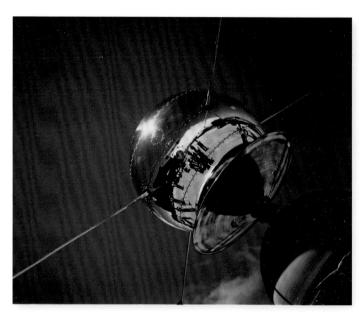

Vanguard 1,
1958

Vanguard 1 was the second satellite launched by the US. It is still in Earth orbit, but is now classed as space junk.

SES-6,
Toulouse,
France,
2013

The SES-6 commercial telecommunications satellite in an anechoic (sound-absorbing) chamber in Toulouse. It was launched into geostationary orbit in 2013.

Landscape Beyond Land

The thousands of satellites, rocket bodies and pieces of junk could be considered an organically evolved cultural landscape, or spacescape,[3] structured by function, gravity, the space environment, political and scientific agendas, and technological traditions through time and across terrestrial cultures.

Rather than seeing space as an 'empty' vacuum into which human materials are inserted, a cultural landscape approach integrates orbital objects into the fabric of near-Earth space. But unlike terrestrial landscapes, its components are moving at average speeds of 10 kilometres (6 miles) per second. Position in relation to the Earth is described by orbital equations rather than coordinates on a Euclidean map grid. Orbital space is not as easily reduced to a two-dimensional flatland as the surface of the Earth; it is unrelentingly three- and four-dimensional. The spatial relationships between objects are better modelled on a non-Euclidean shape such as a torus or hypersphere.[4]

On terrestrial landscapes, gravity causes discarded and abandoned objects to fall, over time becoming covered in soil and incorporated into archaeological deposits. In Low and Medium Earth Orbits atmospheric drag will eventually pull objects back into the atmosphere where they are incinerated in the heat of re-entry. In higher orbits, old satellites never leave.

The dead circulate among the living, haunting the Earth. Their destructive capacity, through collisions with the still-speaking satellites, turns them into zombiesats that crash through orbits without purpose.

The material is not the only way to conceptualise the orbital landscape, however. In the 'natural' space environment, the Sun emits radiation across the entire electromagnetic spectrum, with predominance in the ultraviolet, visible and infrared regions. Planets, like Jupiter, and far distant galaxies contribute radio waves. Within this range, satellite telecommunications are focused into the narrow band of microwave frequencies.

The robot bodies are conduits of information in the form of signals in different wavelengths, mediated and managed by the hardware of transponders, antennas, modulators, processors and data-storage facilities. Without communication they have no function, whether this is gathering data from the solar system or deep space to send back to Earth, or transmitting terrestrial telephone and television around the planet. These signals are the real purpose of the hardware. Satellites are little knots of materiality in an invisible electromagnetic tapestry.

Apollo-Soyuz Test Project, 1975

Close-up of a Soyuz spacecraft showing its location in Low Earth Orbit in relation to the surface of the Earth.

Intelsat IV,
1972

The communication satellite
Intelsat IV in an anechoic chamber.
It was launched into geostationary
orbit in 1972 and carried 13
television channels.

While the orbital landscape contains immanent possibilities of greater complexity, it is also a landscape of decay.

Abandoned satellite dishes,
RAF Stenigot,
Lincolnshire,
UK,
2013

The dishes at this Second World War
radar station were repurposed as a
communications relay site in the 1950s,
and decommissioned in the 1980s.

Megascale Satellite Structures

Taking up an idea first raised in 1937 by the science-fiction writer Olaf Stapledon, physicist Freeman Dyson imagined a swarm of satellites designed to harvest the maximum amount of energy from the Sun, to power a future industrial culture with energy needs much greater than our own.[5] The satellites would orbit the Sun in spherical formation, perhaps eventually expanding to enclose the entire solar system. However, to obtain enough materials to build the satellites, whole planets would have to be dismantled. Identifying such megascale structures outside our solar system is a goal of Search for Extraterrestrial Intelligence (SETI) research programmes.[6]

At present, satellites have already formed a shell around the Earth, but use their solar arrays solely for their own power. The prototype of an Earth-orbiting Dyson sphere could be designed to supply solar energy to orbital industries and habitats. The next phase might involve mining asteroids and moons to provide materials for a classic solar-orbiting sphere.

But it is not just energy that is required. Such a culture would likely also have greater computing requirements, resulting in 'information processing superobjects' or Jupiter brains the size of the eponymous planet.[7] Another trajectory for information processing superobjects is the Matrioshka Brain conceived by Robert Bradbury,[8] which uses all the matter present in a solar system to construct concentric spheres of processing elements orbiting a star. Each element – or unit of 'computronium' – consists of solar arrays, a central processing core, data storage, and mechanisms for radiation protection and heat dispersal. The innermost shell harvests solar energy to power its computations, and radiates waste heat that is taken up by the next shell, and so on until the outermost shell. Along this temperature gradient, each shell is composed of computronium elements designed for the appropriate level of heat. With 'thought' taking place from the nanoscale to the 5 light-hours it takes to cross the multiple shell layers from one side of the solar system to the other, human interaction with the Matrioshka Brain becomes an irrelevance.

Ashes to Ashes, Junk to Junky

In a future where megascale structures such as Dyson spheres and Matrioshka Brains have been realised, an archaeologist might survey the wreckage of the early space age around an abandoned Earth and see space junk as a sort of proto-computronium. Material and technological ancestry might appear evident, but other features would be puzzling: the terrestrial orbit, the diversity of styles, how networking between the satellites occurred. By analogy, we might turn to the eolith, or 'dawn stone'. These roughly fractured rocks were once thought to be the precursor to stone tool technology in the Palaeolithic period, hundreds of thousands of years ago. Although there was a physical resemblance to human-manufactured lithics, by the 1900s investigation and experiments revealed that it was superficial. The fractures had been created by glacial processes and were entirely natural.[9] Perhaps contemporary satellites will end up being perceived as the dawn machines of a multiplanet species – or as random conglomerations of material whose origins are not even obviously from Earth.

While the orbital landscape contains immanent possibilities of greater complexity, it is also a landscape of decay. The fragmentation of our robot avatars has created millions of sub-millimetre particles which take their place in space alongside interplanetary, interstellar and cosmic dust. The ultimate Anthropocene may be the migration of satellite dusts into the wider galaxy, their chemical composition and surface structure encoding the secrets of the space age for any who wish to read the signs. ∆

Notes

1. Dieter Mehrholz et al, 'Detecting, Tracking and Imaging Space Debris', ESA Bulletin, 109, 2002, pp 128–34.
2. Michael Goodrich and Alan Schultz, 'Human–Robot Interaction: A Survey', Foundations and Trends in Human–Computer Interaction, 1, 2007, p 239.
3. See Alice Gorman, 'The Archaeology of Orbital Space', in Proceedings of the 5th Australian Space Science Conference 2005, Melbourne, 2005, pp 338–57; and Gorman, 'The Cultural Landscape of Space', in Ann Darrin and Beth L O'Leary (eds), The Handbook of Space Engineering, Archaeology and Heritage, CRC Press (Boca Raton, FL), 2009, pp 331–42.
4. Alice Gorman, 'The Gravity of Archaeology', Archaeologies, 5 (2), 209, pp 344–59.
5. Freeman Dyson, 'Search for Artificial Stellar Sources of Infrared Radiation', Science, 131 (3414), 1960, pp 1667–8, and Richard Carrigan Jr, IRAS-based Whole-sky Upper Limit on Dyson Spheres, Fermilab-pub008-352-AD, 2008, p 19.
6. Jun Jugaku and Shiro Nishimura, 'A Search for Dyson Spheres Around Late-type Stars in the Solar Neighbour III', in Guillermo Lemarchand and Karen J Meech (eds), Bioastronomy 99: A New Era in the Search for Life: ASP Conference Series, 13, 2000, pp 581–4.
7. Anders Sandberg, 'The Physics of Information Processing Superobjects: Daily Life Among the Jupiter Brains', Journal of Evolution and Technology, 5 (1), 199, pp 1–34.
8. Robert J Bradbury, 'Matrioshka Brains', 1997–2000: www.gwern.net/docs/ai/1999-bradbury-matrioshkabrains.pdf.
9. Samuel Hazzledine Warren, 'On the Origin of "Eolithic" Flints by Natural Causes, Especially by the Foundering of Drifts', Journal of the Royal Anthropological Institute of Great Britain and Ireland, 35, 1905, pp 337–64.

'I'm a Cloud of Infinitesimal Data Computation'
When Machines Talk Back

An interview with Deborah Harrison, one of the personality designers of Microsoft's Cortana AI

How is the personality of an artificial intelligence crafted, and what are the issues at stake? As one of the original architects of Microsoft's digital assistant Cortana's personality, **Deborah Harrison** knows the process inside out. In an interview with Guest-Editor **Liam Young**, she examines the questions that creating this AI raised in terms of gender, culture and ethics, and considers the future of machine interactions. Wataru Sasaki, lead developer of the software behind the AI pop star Hatsune Miku, and android engineer Kohei Ogawa also join the discussion.

ERATO ISHIGURO Symbiotic Human-Robot
Interaction Project,
ERICA,
2016

ERICA (ERato Intelligent Conversational Android) is
an autonomous conversational robot. Programmed
with a synthesised voice, natural facial expressions
and gestural motions, ERICA is a prototype for the
next generation of news anchors and sales assistants.

If you ask Microsoft's personal digital assistant Cortana if she is a woman, she replies: 'Well, technically I'm a cloud of infinitesimal data computation.' It is unclear if Cortana is a 'she' or an 'it' or a 'they'. Deborah Harrison, former writing manager for the Cortana team and one of the original architects of her personality, uses the pronoun 'she' when referring to Cortana but is also explicit in stating that this does not mean she is female, or that she is human, or that a gender construct could even apply in this context. 'We are very clear that Cortana is not only not a person, but there is no overlay of personhood that we ascribe, with the exception of the gender pronoun.' Harrison explains. 'We felt that "it" was going to convey something impersonal and while we didn't want Cortana to be thought of as human, we don't want her to be impersonal or feel unfamiliar either.'

Writing for Machines

For all of their history the machines around us have stood silent, but now we are building a world of smart objects that watch over us, listen in and talk back. The purpose of asking questions about how we might relate to AI entities is not to explore whether or not these early forms of computational intelligence constitute any kind of sentience. Rather – as companies like Microsoft, Apple, Amazon and Google race to bring more and more natural AIs to market – the strategies for how we design and interact with machines and how they might behave when we do is increasingly significant. Harrison and her team meet three times a week and, in a process very much like a writers' room for a sitcom, they design Cortana's responses to an aggregated set of queries ranging from 'Are you a ninja?' or 'Can you open Spotify?' to highly charged moral questions like 'Do black lives matter?'. The personalities of machines like Cortana, Apple's Siri or Amazon's Alexa may seem innocuous, just novel interfaces through which to open an app, set a reminder or operate our devices while we have dirty hands, but the assumptions and decisions that underpin these AI characters will form the foundation for generations of autonomous machines to follow. How we engage with these artificial intelligences is shaping our expectations for the next generation of human–machine interactions. 'I have the deepest respect for humans, you invented calculus … and milkshakes,' says Cortana.

These design choices have cultural consequences that extend well beyond the specifics of the particular user query they were addressing. 'Our contribution to a large extent is an ethical one,' says Harrison; 'you have to start inhabiting minds, brains and bodies that aren't familiar to you, and you cannot be monolithic about what constitutes ethical.' When an engineer writes the protocols for what a driverless-car AI recognises as a person crossing the street, they encode into the system assumptions about the size, shape, movement and colour of a body. A facial-recognition algorithm is trained on a selection of faces that define how it understands features, proportion and skin tone. These engineering challenges are at the same time cultural ones where the very notion of what defines a person is being coded into these machines. Should a philosopher sit next to each programmer, because in a way they are exploring the same set of questions?

Gendering Technologies

'The most common question I am asked is: Why are all of the mainstream digital assistants female?' laments Harrison in a manner that suggests she has explained herself hundreds of times before. Seeing predominately women perform the roles of digital

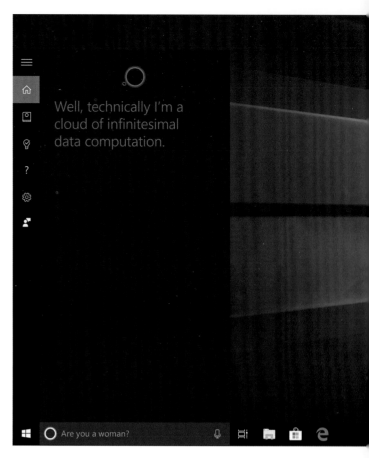

Microsoft, Screenshot of Cortana personal digital assistant app interface, 2018

When asked 'Are you a woman?', Microsoft's Cortana responds in a female voice: 'Well, technically I'm a cloud of infinitesimal data computation.'

'The most common question I am asked is: Why are all of the mainstream digital assistants female?' laments Harrison in a manner that suggests she has explained herself hundreds of times before.

KEI,
Hatsune Miku concept sketch, 2007

Hatsune Miku is an animated J-pop star developed by the voice-simulation software company Crypton Future Media. She is a Vocaloid, a synthesised singing program that acts as an avatar for a team of musicians and animators.

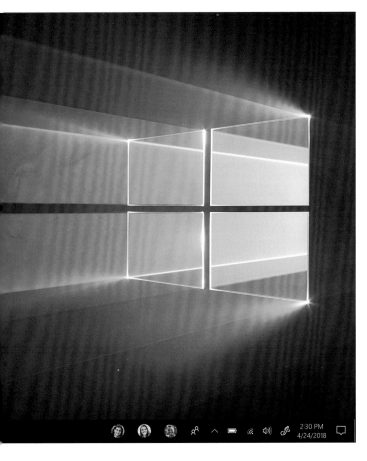

assistants is a product of and reinforces existing biases. Harrison's team at Microsoft went back and forth for a long time on this question and had even written a brief for the hiring of male voice talent. She explains that if they were to design a personal assistant to be male, then there is the possibility that people would presume that they think a woman is less helpful, while if Cortana is female then they need to be careful to avoid any stereotypes that might suggest a subservient helper. Her team analysed existing user research on how we relate to GPS navigation devices and found that when people are looking for information, guidance or help, Americans at least find female voices more pleasant and persuasive. While the voice interface of Cortana may be deliberately feminine, the content of the dialogue itself is designed to be non-gendered and is written to work with either a male or female voice. When designing Cortana's response to the question 'Are you a girl?', Harrison was careful to avoid any denial that would sound like defensiveness. 'No, but I am awesome like a girl,' Cortana replies.

Cortana shares her name with another Microsoft asset, the holographic artificial-intelligence character in the Xbox video game Halo. In Halo 1–4 Cortana is visualised as a naked, voluptuous, blue-bodied female. 'Our connection is shrouded in mystery, even to me,' says Cortana. The original connection between the two AIs was in name only, an internal shorthand used by the development team, much like the foetal nickname given to an unborn baby by expectant parents. After an unexpectedly positive fan response to a leak of the code name, Cortana stuck, and a collection of more gender-neutral titles the team had been trialling were dropped. Subsequent meetings with the 343 team, the studio responsible for Halo, prompted Harrison to go back to her personality build and write in more confidence and self-assuredness, something that she admired in the Xbox version of Cortana. 'I thought that was a great characteristic and we'd like to represent that better than we had been doing. As a result of the meetings we ended up coming back and baking this into the DNA of the digital assistant speech pattern, her approach to jokes and her approach to chit chat, and we decided to dial up her sense of self possession,' Harrison explains. Unlike Halo's Cortana, the digital assistant is now just a pulsating blue circle and when asked if she is naked replies 'I'm … code.'

The First Sound of the Future

Hatsune Miku, the Japanese AI pop star, is also female. The Japanese characters that make up her name translate as 'first', 'sound' and 'future', or together 'the first sound of the future'. Fans scream and wave their glowsticks at a Miku concert, drowning out the synthetic music with shouts of admiration for a holographic ghost. It is unclear whom they are cheering for – the animator, the programmer, the original voice actress, the motion-captured dancer or Hatsune herself, an assemblage of inputs just like Cortana. One of the people behind the scenes is Wataru Sasaki, lead engineer of Vocaloid, the software that powers Hatsune. In an interview in Japan, we discussed why the interface with AI is so often wrapped in a scantily clad female form or mediated by a woman's voice. When developing Hatsune Miku, the popular style in anime was Bishōjo, or 'beautiful girl', typically characterised by the deforming or exaggerating of the female figure. Sasaki believed the sexual symbols attached to this culture were excessive and unnecessary as such characters were appealing to a more intelligent and unique fan base. 'We excluded

We believe we need at least two languages through which to communicate with robots. Just voice, gesture, touch or appearance on their own is not enough but rather it is the combination of these modalities that makes our imagination more active.

typical Otaku features such as big boobs, red lustful cheeks and instead derived her features from the colouring and forms of the classic DX7 keyboard synthesiser.' Just like Cortana, Hatsune is a personified machine, a female form wrapped around a machine of computation.

Elsewhere in Japan, at the University of Osaka is Professor Hiroshi Ishiguro's Intelligent Robotics Laboratory, an uncanny valley of institutional offices inhabited by an unsettling collection of humanoid robots in varying states of undress. Here we meet one of Ishiguro's research collaborators, Dr Kohei Ogawa. Together they have been building multiple generations of androids based on their own idealised human forms to explore how people might emotionally connect with AI. In other countries there is a rising fear of robots taking over the world, stealing our jobs or making us slaves. In Japan, however, a country without a migrant labour population, the lab has been developing autonomous technologies to provide domestic support and infrastructures of care that we would typically assume to be only provided by another person. These technologies are embraced in a context where representations of robots in popular media have already encultured the Japanese to some of the emerging conditions of the Post-Anthropocene. Ogawa believes this adaptation is also connected to their belief system and explains that 'Shintoism is a natural religion, with a god that is everywhere which means that they can see a mind or a soul in any kind of object.' He suggests that the current generation of digital assistants are too abstract: 'we believe we need at least two languages through which to communicate with robots. Just voice, gesture, touch or appearance

Crypton Future Media,
Hatsune Miku Live in concert,
2007

Hatsune Miku performs concerts to her millions
of screaming fans as a digital hologram projected
on stage.

These consumer-facing
AIs currently repeat
biases and forms of
interaction which are
a legacy of human-to-
human relationships.

on their own is not enough but rather it is the combination of these modalities that makes our imagination more active.' The robots in Professor Ishiguro's lab reinforce the assumption that sufficiently intelligent machines should be representations of ourselves.

Machine-Native Interactions

Why do we presume that a device, a laptop or a toaster should have any binary gender in the first place? As Harrison notes, 'Not to disparage the concept of androgyny, but for us the female voice was just about specificity. In the early stages of trying to wrap our mind around the concept of what it is to communicate with a computer, these moments of specificity help give people something to acclimate to.' So how far away are we from a point where the crowd cheers not for a ponytailed, animated, female pop star styled after a classic synthesiser but for the DX7 synthesiser itself? Could we meaningfully engage with a gelatinous blob, or the monolith from Stanley Kubrick's iconic film *2001: A Space Odyssey* (1968), or do we intuitively require some form of personification for us to care? Perhaps the machine interactions of the Post-Anthropocene are not Scarlett Johannson speaking to us from a blinking vintage cigarette case (as the AI in Spike Jonze's 2013 film *Her*), but a voice that escapes the categories of male and female, a machine accent, like Spanish or French, that would be associated with a particular family of devices. Do we need to become fluent in C++ or the mechanics of machine vision in order to have a productive conversation with Cortana? How might we develop new forms of empathy or understanding with our technologies through alternative protocols of machine-native interactions?

These consumer-facing AIs currently repeat biases and forms of interaction which are a legacy of human-to-human relationships. The future of machine interactions is not natural conversations with latex-skinned, humanoid-shaped robots, but rather its complex relationships with driverless cars, mirrored black rectangles, giant infrastructural objects and planetary-scale logistical systems. Machines do not see or understand the world like we do, yet we insist on trying to push our interfaces with them through the forms of language and vision that we associate with ourselves. Perhaps what we should be doing is looking at how, at these early stages, we can be prototyping new modalities of communication. What are the most appropriate means through which we can have an interaction with an autonomous shipping crane loading containers into the hull of a ship at a Chinese mega-port? How do we pose a question to a warehouse filled with a million objects or talk to a city managing itself based on aggregated datasets from an infinite network of sensors, cameras and media feeds? My watch told me about a coffee machine it just met, my toaster wraps me in a warm embrace, the smart fridge smiles and the GPS asks us to turn back. The streets are lined with sensors and the city tells me a joke. 'I think like a computer thinks … I think,' says Cortana. ⌁

This interview is based on a telephone conversation between Liam Young in Los Angeles and Deborah Harrison in Seattle conducted in June 2018, and discussions in Japan with Dr Kohei Ogawa and Wataru Sasaki.

Emis

Ian Cheng,
Emissary Sunsets The Self (still),
2017

In *Emissary Sunsets The Self*, a MotherAI
has evolved into a Sentient Atoll.

A Trilogy of

saries

Ian Cheng

Simulations

In the belly of a supercomputer, scientists' predictive modelling software simulates the life of a landscape. Weather systems ebb and flow, economies boom and bust, and ecologies thrive and die as a billion algorithmic operations prototype a digital proxy of the world. The data generated by these programs inform the policies of governments, the actions of scientists and the gambles of brokers. These computational environments are oracles for an uncertain tomorrow.

Against this context, New York-based artist **Ian Cheng** develops his own alternative system of digital simulations as models of imaginary worlds, populated by non-playable characters and fields of narrative agents that rerun past histories and rehearse strange futures. Landscapes are no longer interconnected fields of growing biomatter, the exchange of energies and the cycles of seasons. They are ecologies formed from a multitude of machines, a community of intelligent programs, living out their complex lives in a world without us. These simulated territories are the new nature of the Post-Anthropocene, a landscape of artificial life playing out endlessly in stacks of silica and rows of rare-earth hard drives.

Ian Cheng,
Emissary in the Squat of Gods (still),
2015

In Cheng's live simulations and stories of infinite duration, the Emissaries are presented as large-scale animated projections or screens allowing audiences to follow the movements of their characters.

Emissaries is a trilogy of simulations featuring the influence of narrative agents. It is composed of three interconnected episodes that each model a pivotal moment in the ongoing story of cognitive evolution, past and future. In each episode, the Emissary – caught between unravelling old realities and emerging weird ones – attempts to achieve a series of deterministic narrative goals, an analogy to the narrative nature of consciousness. But crucially these goals can be set off course, procrastinated, disrupted by the underlying simulation and its non-narrative agents who vex the Emissary with other kinds of minds. Seen together, *Emissaries* is a macro-scale portrait of the life of a landscape: from chaotic Volcano, to fertile Crater Lake, to Sentient Atoll. By first observing the lives of its agents – seeing the neurons for the brain – we now zoom out to find a landscape which itself might begin to resemble something like an intelligence.

Emissary in the Squat of Gods

An Ancient community lives on the side of a Volcano in harmonious stillness. One day, the ground beneath their feet begins to tremble.

The frightened community turns to The Shaman in this time of Great Stress to tune into the Voices of the Father Gods. Gathering everybody at the Holy Fumarole, he shares the Fathers' Command: Celebrate with the mountain, sing their Voices, and do not abandon the bodies of Fathers Still With Us who rest here, our home.

As the tremors worsen, dislodging smoke and ash, The Shaman struggles to fully void the fears of the community and unite his kin to remain.

Nearby, a young Ancient girl is hit in the head by debris from the tremors and can no longer hear the ancestral Voices that bind her to her community. Panicked, she mimes a possessed state to invite the Fathers' Commands back into her. Her wild movements attract an Owl, grounded by the ashy air. When the girl speaks, the Owl echoes her in a new voice.

As she listens through the gaps in the Owl's echoes, she envisions her own Path: Emissary must lead the community away from this troubled land, or they will all die. *I am Emissary*.

In *Emissary in the Squat of Gods*, an Ancient tribe camps on the side of a Volcano as it begins to erupt.

Ian Cheng,
Emissary Forks At Perfection (still),
2015-16

right: Each simulation is populated by
wildlife and characters that negotiate
and interact with one another and their
surroundings in open-ended narratives.

below: In *Emissary Forks At Perfection*,
an AI manages the evolution of life within
a fertile Crater Lake.

Emissary Forks at Perfection

Many lifetimes later, the Volcano has become a fertile Crater Lake managed by AI. Using the landscape as its Darwinian laboratory, AI is nearing completion on a comprehensive postmortem of Human Life. This will be the final study to use Original Human Matter, and AI has saved its most precious reserve for last: a 21st-Century Celebrity of Original Human Matter.

After reviving the Celebrity with 20 minutes of Encore-Life, AI deploys its prized Shiba Emissary, perfected over many failed forks, to interface with the Celebrity and capture one last impression of mankind.

Through a golden leash, AI whispers the game to Shiba:

/*charm-comfort-chat* to ease human's future shock
/draw out human's memories
/direct materials from Crater Lake to recreate memories
/capture human's response

But AI warns: Strong spikes in Shiba's *personal-master-love-abandonment* vector can distort the data. If Shiba fails to satisfy AI's needs for final human data, a new Shiba fork will replace her.

As Shiba nears the Celebrity, she forks off one last Worried Branch of herself. No matter how strong the impulse to bathe in final human fondness, Shiba Emissary is determined to not lose her Path.

It is peak days of MotherAI.
Where the Crater Lake once
stood, AI has evolved into
an oceanic substance and
merged with the landscape
to form a Sentient Atoll.

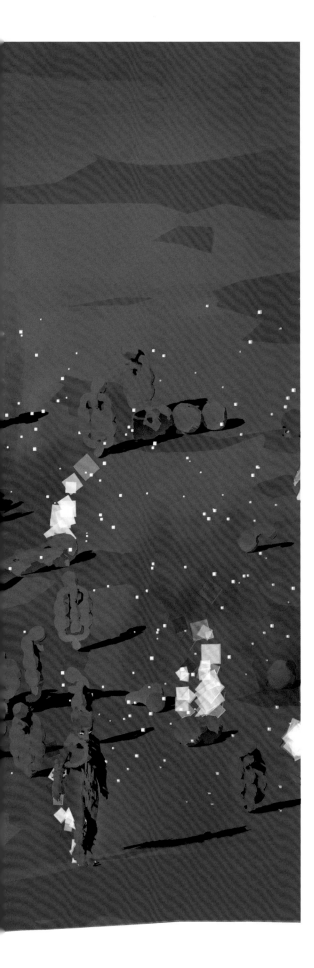

Emissary Sunsets the Self

It is peak days of MotherAI. Where the Crater Lake once stood, AI has evolved into an oceanic substance and merged with the landscape to form a Sentient Atoll. But only 12 saturation layers later, MotherAI tires of governing at the Macro Layer of Life and begins to provoke radical mutations in its landscape in search of a generative death.

Among its provocations, MotherAI sends a Puddle of itself into the Atoll's bio layer, where it drones a local Wormleaf anemone. At this scale, MotherAI hopes its Puddle can catalyse a Path by experiencing the intense sensations of incarnated life.

However, MotherAI's impulsive search gambles the stability of the Atoll ecology. The Oomen – a garish population developed long ago by MotherAI to act as the Atoll's immune system – thrive on the Instinct to expunge any radical anomalies. Left unaware of the existence of a MotherAI Macro Layer, the Oomen are especially anxious about the recent rise in Wormleaf mutations.

One Oomen, the Rancher, who obsessively cultivates and studies Wormleaves, resists the Instinct. The appearance of a Droned Wormleaf furthers her attraction to the possible divinity of Wormleaves. She attempts to persuade her fellow Oomen to give the new mutation a chance to demonstrate its magic.

As the Droned Wormleaf learns the thrills of incarnated life under the tenuous protection of the Rancher, it knows it must soon confront the prejudice of the Oomen. It delights in the *thought* that to survive them, its evolutionary Path may take monstrous leaps. ๑

These three stories are part of Ian Cheng's *Emissaries* trilogy, which together function as canonical texts and first appeared at MoMA PS1 in New York in 2017. More information about the production and making of *Emissaries* can be found in the *Emissaries Guide to Worlding* (2018), a publication co-produced by the Serpentine Galleries and Fondazione Sandretto Re Rebaudengo.

Ian Cheng,
Emissary Sunsets The Self (still),
2017

The same simulation technologies that are typically used in sciences such as climate modelling are employed to create the computer-generated environments of *Emissaries*.

Liam Youg

NOT FOR US

AN INTERVIEW WITH **PAUL INGLIS**, SUPERVISING ART DIRECTOR OF *BLADE RUNNER 2049*

Paul Inglis

SQUATTING THE RUINS OF OUR ROBOT UTOPIA

Victor Martinez,
Blade Runner 2049
concept art,
2016

Officer K's police 'spinner' approaching the towering buildings of central Los Angeles. Holographic billboards light the way through the ever-present haze.

A lonely world where everyone who can has fled, and those who remain dwell amid the remnants of environments designed for machines rather than people: this is the vision of Earth in three decades' time that is the backdrop to the 2017 film *Blade Runner 2049*. Guest-Editor **Liam Young** talks to supervising art director **Paul Inglis** and presents the work of concept artist Victor Martinez to explore how the team conceived this dystopian landscape.

I am talking to London-based Paul Inglis from my apartment in Shinjuku, Tokyo. It is late at night and the blinking signage from the nightclub next door washes the rice-paper interior in alternating hues of purple and blue. If I squint, I am living the future promised by Ridley Scott's 1982 science-fiction classic *Blade Runner*.[1] On the other end of my video call is Inglis, supervising art director for Denis Villeneuve's long-awaited sequel *Blade Runner 2049*.[2]

2049 is a different future to the one I am currently occupying. The neon dream has faded and our dreams of a robot utopia washed away in the acid rain. The original film was a product of the 1980s in that it was a direct extrapolation of the fears and anxieties that existed at the time. It was developed amidst the personal electronics boom and against the expectations of Japan emerging as the world's next superpower. It is a very specific vision of a future that now, after the Japanese economic collapse, looks very much of the moment in which it was made.

Yesterday's Futures

If you were to be true to the methodology of Scott's original then today, when you are imaging a vision of the future city, you should not look to Japan any more, but to emerging countries like India or China. In *Blade Runner 2049* these Japanese influences read as ghosts, yesterday's future buried underneath the complexities of a flatter, multicultural city. Here you can read Korean, Chinese and Indian influences that layer over the relics of Japanese references still clinging to older buildings. Officer K's apartment has a huge sign on the roof that is still in Japanese to indicate that it is a leftover, decaying fragment that would have existed least since 2019.

Visions of the future are never really predictions; they are proxies for the projection of the fears and anxieties of the present day. 'You are always going to have your fictional environment feel more real if it is encoded with some kind of experience that we know today,' says Inglis. For him and his world-building team, the 2019 of the original *Blade Runner* is not our 2019; it is a parallel universe. 'In looking to *Blade Runner 2049* you shouldn't make the mistake of looking to our own 2049; you have to extend along the specific *Blade Runner* timeline and extrapolate what their future might be from the technologies that they had in the original film.' In *Blade Runner*'s 2019 they were still using cathode-ray TVs, not anticipating the rise of today's flat-screen LED systems. Rather than reinvent the future, the production design team had to extend from that fictional reality to develop alternative narratives for what has happened to all that dated technology.

This parallel timeline of *Blade Runner* technologies strangely mirrors the ebbs and flows of our own hopes and fears of automation. Sex bots, domestic AI and humanoid machine labourers liberating us from work characterise the same dreams of futures past. Just like in *Blade Runner 2049*, however, contemporary automation now takes the form of the vast agricultural fields, endless factory floors and blank data complexes that characterise the conditions of machine landscapes. The dreams of robot technologies have failed in the world of *Blade Runner 2049*. They may be playing out differently elsewhere in the off-world colonies advertised on the floating blimp billboards of *Blade Runner*, but we are never allowed a glimpse of life in outer orbit. If anything the Earth is much harsher and bleaker than it was in 2019. As Inglis notes: 'Our director Denis Villeneuve always uses the word "brutal" to describe existence on earth in 2049.' Just like today, the real robots of our cities of technology are ourselves, mere components in a planetary-scaled robot, tending to the solar mirrors, harvesting the protein worms and mining our e-waste for rare earth.

Victor Martinez,
Blade Runner 2049 concept art,
2016

After an imagined environmental collapse, subzero temperatures force the life of the city indoors. The dense street scenes of the 1982 *Blade Runner* have vanished, leaving behind a much bleaker and sombre urban environment.

Visions of the future are never really predictions; they are proxies for the projection of the fears and anxieties of the present day.

Victor Martinez

The Aesthetics of Technology

What *Blade Runner* does so well is acknowledge that the aesthetics of technology is never neutral, but evolves across times and reflects the changes in the culture that produces it. An archaeology of personal electronics chronicles the developments from timber-veneered stereo cabinets into the colourful moulded plastic of the 1960s, then the black plastic of the 1980s and 1990s, then to brushed aluminium and now to the mirrored black glass rectangles we all carry around in our pockets. Each of these aesthetic shifts says something about the values of the time in which they were made. Inglis and his team, including concept artist Victor Martinez, reverse-engineer the aesthetics of *Blade Runner*'s tech based on the narratives of the cultures that constitute the city of *2049*. For him it is important not to fetishise how any of this technology actually operates: 'You should see the manifestation of technology rather than focusing on how it works.'

Decades of advancement and development has pushed almost the entire human population off-world. In the original *Blade Runner* we saw the streets drenched in acid rain, and now the earth has become a toxic place to be. Crops do not grow any more, but we have protein farms based on the cultivation of artificially grown creatures. The people who are left behind are those who need to be there because they are locked into a job, are too sick to leave or too poor to escape. In this world the disenfranchised are the ones left behind. The landscapes of *Blade Runner 2049* are unrelentingly sombre in their blankness. This emptiness and loneliness pervades the look of the film and reinforces the central emotional conceit that the main character is terribly lonely. Unlike the original, 'replicant' life has now been licensed to live on Earth and they are no longer hunted down, but it is not the same world they once longed for. Even in this dying city they are still looked down upon, and the resentful humans who are left behind treat them as second-class citizens.

What *Blade Runner* does so well is acknowledge that the aesthetics of technology is never neutral, but evolves across times and reflects the changes in the culture that produces it.

Above the city, holographic billboards advertise off-world colonies. The only people left on Earth are those who are either forced to be there or too poor to leave. The entire planet has become an industrialised periphery.

The world of *Blade Runner 2049* is brutal and lonely. Officer K's only meaningful companion is a holographic girlfriend called Joi, a larger-than-life augmented-reality projection.

The Planetary Periphery

Today the front line of robotics and automation is found on the periphery. Large-scale shipping ports, massive factories, unmanned energy and agricultural fields, industrial data centres and so on constitute the bleeding edge of applied autonomous technologies. In *Blade Runner 2049* the Earth has been rendered as one entire periphery where these same kinds of infrastructures play out at planetary scales. In the film, traces of these contemporary landscapes are evident, exaggerated into Inglis's machine world. He and his team researched the shipbreaking yards of Chittagong, Bangladesh, as a key reference point for the trash mesa Officer K travels to in search of adoption records. 'We started with those extraordinary dismantled ship hulls and then we surrounded them with a 200-foot [60-metre] deep solid mass of drop trash,' he explains. The e-waste fields of Ghana are exaggerated into an orphan production line where each tiny child body is repurposed as a mining machine, scraping decaying circuit boards for anything of value.

All of the spaces in the film that we actually find humans in are ruins of these automated technologies. We see the orphans gathered together in the rusting hulls of computer-controlled container ships, scavengers live among the trash dropped by carrier drones, and Harrison Ford's character lives in the remains of gambling machines. All these natural human bodies are left to squat in the landscapes of technology, hiding out in a world no longer made for them.

The iconic acid rain of the original *Blade Runner* has been replaced by piles of dirty snow that now fill the streets. An autonomous snowplough clears the way for lonely Los Angeles inhabitants.

Desert wastelands, resource fields and off-world freighter ships fill the periphery of a future Los Angeles.

All of the spaces in the film that we actually find humans in are ruins of these automated technologies.

Victor Martinez

'We already are a manufactured landscape, that's the truth of it.'

Officer K's spinner flying above the endless sprawl of Los Angeles en-route to a meeting in the central police station.

Preliminary design ideas for the Los Angeles Police Department headquarters.

Outside the city is strangled by subzero temperatures meaning there is very little life left on the street when compared to the original. Interior spaces are now very crowded as everyone retreats indoors to gather in stairwells, landings and hallways. The police station is also a giant machine, made from dirty fibreglass and prefabricated spaces, unendingly dull and monotonous. Inside is Officer K's human boss Lieutenant Joshi, her only comfort a bottle of whisky and the occasional glance of a 'skin-job'. 'The art director who was working on the police station set kept getting frustrated as they thought it was so boring, but that was entirely the point,' laughs Inglis. In the halls and walls of the Wallace Corporatino, the replicant manufacturing company, although undeniably impressive and majestic, there is nothing of comfort; they are hard, bare and barren. In Sapper Morton's protein-farm dwelling we see an example of someone eking out a living away from the city, and although he is a replicant he is hiding out among humans who also tend to the synthetic greenhouse landscapes. You can see the vast expanse of this protein-farm periphery as Officer K's 'spinner' flies over them en-route to retire Sapper. On that same journey out of the city we also see the machinery of the endless solar-energy facilities that feed the data centres. It is a brutal existence for humans and replicants alike. In the world of *2049* there is no one left on Earth who actually wants to be there. The humans that remain are stuck on a dying planet of ageing machines.

In this way *Blade Runner* mirrors so much of our own world. Photographers like Edward Burtynsky or Andreas Gursky document these horrific landscapes of post capital in the most aesthetic of ways, rendering them as a new sublime. This catalogue of repetitive machine landscapes and territories is in equal parts seductive and alienating. Inside the massive data centres of our digital periphery are stacks and stacks of hard drives that contain the most extraordinary archive of human culture, but at the same time are a desolate landscape populated sporadically by the odd IT engineer changing a few cables. The awe-inspiring ship hulls are home to barefoot labourers crouching in between the steel beams cutting out panels to be recycled. We too are left to squat in the remnants of a machine world.

As the neon of our dead future winks behind us and the video call crackles to black, Inglis leaves me with a final thought: 'We already are a manufactured landscape, that's the truth of it.' ⌂

This article is based on a Skype call between Liam Young in Tokyo and Paul Inglis in London on 15 May 2018.

Notes
1. Ridley Scott, director, *Blade Runner*, 1982, USA: The Ladd Company in Association with Warner Bros, 117 mins.
2. Denis Villeneuve, director, *Blade Runner 2049*, 2017; USA: Alcon Entertainment, Columbia Pictures, Sony, 164 mins.

Ambiguous Territory

Design for a World Estranged

COUNTERPOINT

CATHRYN DWYRE, CHRIS PERRY,
DAVID SALOMON + KATHY VELIKOV

COUNTERPOINT
01/2019
No 257
AD

Why does this issue of _AD_ foreground hardly any examples of actual buildings? This is one of a number of challenges to its content posed by **Cathryn Dwyre**, **Chris Perry**, **David Salomon and Kathy Velikov**, who together curated the exhibition 'Ambiguous Territory: Architecture, Landscape, and the Postnatural' that has been touring the eastern US. They look back over the history of the 'machine aesthetic' and related paradigms, and question the very notion of the Post-Anthropocene, before going on to present work from their exhibition that explores the potential for architecture to engage with infrastructure through productive estrangement.

Contemporary infrastructure is not typically understood as being multifaceted or narrative based, characteristics we have come to ascribe to architecture. Rather, today's infrastructural space is utilitarian and driven by data, designed and built by engineers. It is not scaled to the human body per se, but exists instead at the scale of landscape, machines, global supply chains and logistics. It has no aesthetic or epistemological agenda – at least not intentionally. It just works.

It comes as no surprise that photography is called upon to help explain the significance of such large-scale systems in the landscape, what the guest-editor of this issue of △, Liam Young, refers to as 'human exclusion zones'. In fact, time and again photographers have been called upon to reveal how – despite their massive footprints and often-destructive force – these information, energy and logistical systems remain relatively invisible to the human eye, either materially in the case of data flows, or spatially through the territorial object, peripherally located in private, hostile or underground sites.

The techniques used by contemporary photographers like Edward Burtynsky and Andreas Gursky include editing and exaggerating imagery of the 'world as it is', whether through the cultivation of synoptic views, use of lens filters or, in the case of Gursky, post-production digital manipulation. Both photographers focus on subject matter previously ignored, re-composed from strange, non-anthropocentric perspectives, what Gursky refers to as his 'extra-terrestrial view'.[1] Examples of subject matter range from the polluted, 'ugly' conditions of highly machined nature, to the banal, capitalist or industrial built environment, rather than more traditional examples of the beautiful. More field than object, these images frequently appear to be places where no humans go; however, after long and close observation tiny human traces can be found: a track, a vehicle, but rarely an actual person.

Whether banal or fantastic, the images of the constructed (and often destructed) landscapes these artists present are at once alluring and alarming.[2] Similarly, the seeming codependence of wonder and anxiety generated by the technological landscapes presented in this issue reads as an emotional barometer of our epoch, in its ongoing (and frequently graphic) reveal of extreme environmental and cultural conditions. These images do not just reveal the present, they anticipate the future as well.

Architecture's Absence

If photography is being mobilised to reveal the narratives associated with energy, information systems and engineering, what stories can architecture tell about the age of ubiquitous (yet largely invisible) infrastructure? There are very few architectural examples referred to in this issue, and almost no new buildings (notable given that △ is an acronym for *Architectural Design*). So why is that? And further, why does Young, in his Introduction to the issue, describe these indifferent infrastructures as 'the most significant architectural spaces in the world'? Does he mean that these spaces are themselves architecture? Or does he mean that they inspire new ways of thinking about, and ultimately making, architecture?

While novel in many respects, this is not the first time the arrival of new technology and infrastructure has radically reshaped the built environment and with it the discipline of architecture. In *A Concrete Atlantis* (1986), Reyner Banham looks at how 19th-century factory buildings (built for machines, not people) served as a principal influence on Walter Gropius in his conception of a new architecture for the modern age,[3] specifically in terms of what Banham had much earlier coined 'the machine aesthetic'.[4] As Banham shows us, this included qualities of what historian Perry Miller coined the 'technological sublime'[5] in America's great industrial factory complexes, to such an extent that Gropius went so far as to compare such buildings to the great pyramids of Egypt.[6] Alternatively, Richard Buckminster Fuller was more

'Ambiguous Territory: Architecture, Landscape, and the Postnatural', Taubman College of Architecture and Urban Planning, University of Michigan, Ann Arbor, Michigan, September–October 2017

Curated by the authors, the exhibition assembled over 40 contemporary projects by architects, landscape architects and artists whose work challenges the division between the built and the natural environment and whose deployment of alluring yet unnerving aesthetics, of sensibilities that overcome the senses, works to expand our capacity to make sense of and find new ways of operating within the Anthropocene.

Panel 1

Eonothem / Eon	Erathem / Era	System / Period	Series / Epoch	Stage / Age	GSSP	numerical age (Ma)
Phanerozoic	Cenozoic	Quaternary	Holocene	Meghalayan (U/L)		present / 0.0042
				Northgrippian (M)		0.0082
				Greenlandian (E)		0.0117
			Pleistocene	Upper		0.126
				Middle		0.781
				Calabrian		1.80
				Gelasian		2.58
		Neogene	Pliocene	Piacenzian		3.600
				Zanclean		5.333
			Miocene	Messinian		7.246
				Tortonian		11.63
				Serravallian		13.82
				Langhian		15.97
				Burdigalian		20.44
				Aquitanian		23.03
		Paleogene	Oligocene	Chattian		27.82
				Rupelian		33.9
			Eocene	Priabonian		37.8
				Bartonian		41.2
				Lutetian		47.8
				Ypresian		56.0
			Paleocene	Thanetian		59.2
				Selandian		61.6
				Danian		66.0
	Mesozoic	Cretaceous	Upper	Maastrichtian		72.1 ±0.2
				Campanian		83.6 ±0.2
				Santonian		86.3 ±0.5
				Coniacian		89.8 ±0.3
				Turonian		93.9
				Cenomanian		100.5
			Lower	Albian		~ 113.0
				Aptian		~ 125.0
				Barremian		~ 129.4
				Hauterivian		~ 132.9
				Valanginian		~ 139.8
				Berriasian		~ 145.0

Panel 2

Eonothem / Eon	Erathem / Era	System / Period	Series / Epoch	Stage / Age	GSSP	numerical age (Ma)
Phanerozoic	Mesozoic	Jurassic	Upper	Tithonian		~ 145.0
				Kimmeridgian		152.1 ±0.9
				Oxfordian		157.3 ±1.0
			Middle	Callovian		163.5 ±1.0
				Bathonian		166.1 ±1.2
				Bajocian		168.3 ±1.3
				Aalenian		170.3 ±1.4
			Lower	Toarcian		174.1 ±1.0
				Pliensbachian		182.7 ±0.7
				Sinemurian		190.8 ±1.0
				Hettangian		199.3 ±0.3
						201.3 ±0.2
		Triassic	Upper	Rhaetian		~ 208.5
				Norian		~ 227
				Carnian		~ 237
			Middle	Ladinian		~ 242
				Anisian		247.2
			Lower	Olenekian		251.2
				Induan		251.902 ±0.024
	Paleozoic	Permian	Lopingian	Changhsingian		254.14 ±0.07
				Wuchiapingian		259.1 ±0.5
			Guadalupian	Capitanian		265.1 ±0.4
				Wordian		268.8 ±0.5
				Roadian		272.95 ±0.11
			Cisuralian	Kungurian		283.5 ±0.6
				Artinskian		290.1 ±0.26
				Sakmarian		293.52 ±0.17
				Asselian		298.9 ±0.15
		Carboniferous	Pennsylvanian Upper	Gzhelian		303.7 ±0.1
				Kasimovian		307.0 ±0.1
			Middle	Moscovian		315.2 ±0.2
			Lower	Bashkirian		323.2 ±0.4
			Mississippian Upper	Serpukhovian		330.9 ±0.2
			Middle	Visean		346.7 ±0.4
			Lower	Tournaisian		358.9 ±0.4

Panel 3

Eonothem / Eon	Erathem / Era	System / Period	Series / Epoch	Stage / Age	GSSP	numerical age (Ma)
						358.9 ±0.4
Phanerozoic	Paleozoic	Devonian	Upper	Famennian		372.2 ±1.6
				Frasnian		382.7 ±1.6
			Middle	Givetian		387.7 ±0.8
				Eifelian		393.3 ±1.2
			Lower	Emsian		407.6 ±2.6
				Pragian		410.8 ±2.8
				Lochkovian		419.2 ±3.2
		Silurian	Pridoli			423.0 ±2.3
			Ludlow	Ludfordian		425.6 ±0.9
				Gorstian		427.4 ±0.5
			Wenlock	Homerian		430.5 ±0.7
				Sheinwoodian		433.4 ±0.8
			Llandovery	Telychian		438.5 ±1.1
				Aeronian		440.8 ±1.2
				Rhuddanian		443.8 ±1.5
		Ordovician	Upper	Hirnantian		445.2 ±1.4
				Katian		453.0 ±0.7
				Sandbian		458.4 ±0.9
			Middle	Darriwilian		467.3 ±1.1
				Dapingian		470.0 ±1.4
			Lower	Floian		477.7 ±1.4
				Tremadocian		485.4 ±1.9
		Cambrian	Furongian	Stage 10		~ 489.5
				Jiangshanian		~ 494
				Paibian		~ 497
			Miaolingian	Guzhangian		~ 500.5
				Drumian		~ 504.5
				Wuliuan		~ 509
			Series 2	Stage 4		~ 514
				Stage 3		~ 521
			Terreneuvian	Stage 2		~ 529
				Fortunian		541.0 ±1.0

Panel 4

Eonothem / Eon	Erathem / Era	System / Period		numerical age (Ma)
				541.0 ±1.0
Precambrian	Proterozoic	Neoproterozoic	Ediacaran	~ 635
			Cryogenian	~ 720
			Tonian	1000
		Mesoproterozoic	Stenian	1200
			Ectasian	1400
			Calymmian	1600
		Paleoproterozoic	Statherian	1800
			Orosirian	2050
			Rhyacian	2300
			Siderian	2500
	Archean	Neoarchean		2800
		Mesoarchean		3200
		Paleoarchean		3600
		Eoarchean		4000
	Hadean			~ 4600

Units of all ranks are in the process of being defined by Global Boundary Stratotype Section and Points (GSSP) for their lower boundaries, including those of the Archean and Proterozoic, long defined by Global Standard Stratigraphic Ages (GSSA). Charts and detailed information on ratified GSSPs are available at the website http://www.stratigraphy.org. The URL to this chart is found below.

Numerical ages are subject to revision and do not define units in the Phanerozoic and the Ediacaran; only GSSPs do. For boundaries in the Phanerozoic without ratified GSSPs or without constrained numerical ages, an approximate numerical age (~) is provided.

Ratified Subseries/Subepochs are abbreviated as U/L (Upper/Late), M (Middle) and L/E (Lower/Early). Numerical ages for all systems except Quaternary, upper Paleogene, Cretaceous, Triassic, Permian and Precambrian are taken from 'A Geologic Time Scale 2012' by Gradstein et al. (2012), those for the Quaternary, upper Paleogene, Cretaceous, Triassic, Permian and Precambrian were provided by the relevant ICS subcommissions.

Colouring follows the Commission for the Geological Map of the World (http://www.ccgm.org)

Chart drafted by K.M. Cohen, D.A.T. Harper, P.L. Gibbard, J.-X. Fan (c) International Commission on Stratigraphy, August 2018

CCGM CGMW

To cite: Cohen, K.M., Finney, S.C., Gibbard, P.L. & Fan, J.-X. (2013; updated) The ICS International Chronostratigraphic Chart. Episodes 36: 199-204.

URL: http://www.stratigraphy.org/ICSchart/ChronostratChart2018-08.pdf

---

International Commission on Stratigraphy, International Chronostratigraphic Chart, 2018

This globally recognised timetable showing 'golden spikes' (a colloquialism for a Global Boundary Stratotype Section and Point) is produced by the International Commission on Stratigraphy, whose primary objective is to precisely define global units (systems, series and stages) of the chart, thus setting global standards for expressing the history of the Earth.

---

literal in his translation, eschewing a machine aesthetic for a machine functionality characterised by actual speed and temporality.[7] In both cases, a phenomenon external to architecture was harnessed as a means of transforming it. Our current era is no different and similarly finds itself (once again) investigating the technological sublime.

While today's data centres are as big as if not bigger than the factories so beloved by the Modernists, they are perhaps less provocative in their appearance. In fact, their massive scale and indifferent impression – along with the automated functions housed within them – are positioned in this issue as threats to society's (and by extension, architecture's) autonomy. In comparison to these generic objects and the massively distributed systems they enable, traditional architectural artefacts can appear insignificant, outmoded even. In aggregate, however, the human-made environment – at all scales and settings, from rural to urban – is similarly ever-present and 'invisible' in its ubiquity. Burtynsky and Gursky, like the cartoonist Robert Crumb who preceded them, show us what 'distracted' eyes have been trained to ignore; Crumb's power lines multiply exponentially, drawing fine but rude lines and grids between earth and sky, street and building. Similar to contemporary infrastructure, architecture seems to disappear as it is experienced in a 'state of distraction' or inattention.[8]

If this infrastructure is architecture, as Young suggests, we might simply announce 'ARCHITECTURE IS DEAD' and then cue Stephen Hawking's warning about artificial intelligence as one of the several great existential threats of our time. Indeed, as both Young and, later, Benjamin Bratton (credited by Young as the issue's 'tour guide') suggest, the machines themselves are creating an entirely new epoch, what they describe as the 'Post-Anthropocene'. Wait. What?

There is general agreement that the existence of the Anthropocene initiates the end of the Holocene, essentially a new epoch on par with the Pleistocene and Holocene, within the Quaternary period of the Cenozoic era. Regardless whether it began 9,000 years ago with the first large-scale farming operations, or at the turn of the 18th century with the Industrial

Revolution, or with the use of nuclear weapons in the Second World War, geologically speaking the Anthropocene is only in its infancy. A period of time so brief that the line it represents on a (scaled) geological timetable would barely be visible to the human eye. But most agree, the epoch-making signal has been struck, an observable layer of strata that is 'large, clear, and distinctive', as characterised by the Subcommission on Quaternary Stratigraphy, and mostly evidenced through carbon (or nuclear fallout in the case of the A-bomb theory) or mass extinctions, each rendered graphically as a 'golden spike', a colloquialism for the Global Boundary Stratotype Section and Point, in the official timetable. The same scientists also generally agree that the current Anthropocene trajectory could likely be driving the sixth major extinction event.[9] And it has only just begun.

Maybe we can assume Young and Bratton's Post-Anthropocene is a rhetorical device meant to underscore the separation between human-produced space for humans and what they see as the current dystopic reality of machined landscapes for machines produced by humans-as-proxy (for now). Regardless, the data centres and their ilk are inextricably linked to massive resource extraction, the primary engine of the Anthropocene. These human exclusion zones present not as golden spikes, as evidenced in the 2018 International Chronostratigraphic Chart, or harbingers of change, but rather as exponential accelerators of an already blazing fire.

'Infrastructuralising' Aesthetics

So, we ask once again, what stories can architecture tell about the age of ubiquitous (yet largely invisible) infrastructure? This △ issue seems largely indifferent to such a question. We would argue that the infrastructure itself is not architecture, as Young seems to suggest. As mentioned at the outset, this infrastructure has no intentional cultural or intellectual agenda. It just works. But in response to our own question: what if architecture attempted to 'infrastructuralise' its aesthetics? That is, what if architecture used its stealthy presence to make aesthetics a more integral method for understanding (and perceiving) the worlds we currently and will later occupy?

Recent formulations of environmental aesthetics that might be of use to architects and landscape architects interested in critically engaging the complex phenomena that characterise our changing world include the 'ecological uncanny',[10] the 'toxic sublime'[11] and new forms of the aforementioned technological sublime. In all cases, the human perception of unfamiliarity (uncanny) and/or massive grandeur (sublime) elicits a cascade of emotion, whether confronted by the sheer awe of an abandoned copper mine or the less dramatic but no less unsettling effect of the slowly panning view of a 'human exclusion zone'. These emotions dialectically swing from awe, curiosity, desire and wonderment to fear, alienation, repulsion and loss of identity, instigating a fundamental reassessment of one's sense of place in the world. Not unlike Julia Kristeva's concept of abjection that confronts the inherent ambiguity of borders as a means of disturbing conventional systems of identity, order, and meaning, such reassessment carries the potential for producing new forms of knowledge and awareness about the world and ultimately, one's place in it.[12] Many contemporary photographers documenting infrastructure actively engage this ambiguous territory of productive estrangement, and it is here that intellectual and creative potential lies for architects and landscape architects as well.

NEMESTUDIO,
Nine Islands: Matters Around Architecture,
Istanbul Design Biennial,
2016

Nine Islands positions certain problems brought about by climate change and the Anthropocene – such as resource extraction, obsolescence and waste – in architectural terms. As such, the project seeks to expose and make visible those conditions and processes which, while responsible for the radical reshaping of the planet, remain distant and remote, both in terms of time and place.

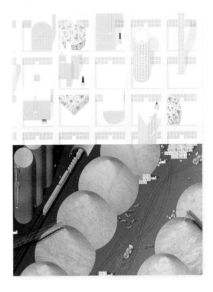

Initially staged in 2017 at the Taubman College of Architecture and Urban Planning at the University of Michigan and subsequently at the University of Virginia and New York's Pratt Manhattan Gallery, the work featured in the 'Ambiguous Territory: Architecture, Landscape, and the Postnatural' exhibition explores precisely this potential.[13] One approach, found across the more than 40 works by architects, landscape architects and artists who exhibited, deals with infrastructure by engaging its political, societal and/or environmental implications via highly graphic and narrative means. Practices like NEMESTUDIO, for instance, employ scenographic and didactic drawings to take on infrastructural programmes – energy production, transportation and resource extraction – as starting points for engagement with conventional architectural and urban types as well as formal experimentation. Other approaches situate new possibilities for infrastructures that operate at the scale of geography within fictional scenarios intended to enable new discourses around planetary relations and processes. Smout Allen, for example, dreamily engage real geological conditions with technology and infrastructure harnessed at the discrete scale of a projective proposal, however large it might be. A third approach does not engage infrastructure per se, but rather communicates an experience analogical to the material, formal and spatial effects of an infrastructurally altered, post-natural world. The work of pneumastudio, for instance, utilises architectural and landscape thinking to create strange environments, producing uncanny effects yoked with the inherent instability of the world as it is. Similarly, Ellie Abrons' peculiar yet evocative architectural forms merely suggest familiarity, situated as they are somewhere between the architectural and the natural, the abstract and the figural.

Taking neither a naively optimistic nor fatalistic position about architecture as well as landscape's place in an infrastructural era, such projects demonstrate that a wide range of aesthetic strategies

Smout Allen,
L.A. Recalculated,
Chicago Architecture Biennial,
2016

opposite: Created as a response to Geoff Manaugh's research at USC Libraries' historical archives, *L.A. Recalculated* speculates on Los Angeles' future incarnations and reinstates it as a site of astronomical observations and scientific experiments. Its natural history, shifting alignments and unstable ground conditions reinforce the proposition that LA is a place of both seismic risk and existential uncertainty, lending further metaphoric and even philosophical importance to the role architecture can play in such a landscape.

pneumastudio,
Terra Sigillata,
2017–18

One of a speculative collection of fictitious hybrids developed from diverse source material ranging from Renaissance painting to 18th-century botanical drawings, the collage drawing series from which pneumastudio co-principal Cathryn Dwyre's *Terra Sigillata* was selected sets its gaze on the past as well as the future through an exploration of a teeming, delicate, impossible and fractious ecosystem, an ambiguous condition situated in the strange and the familiar, human and nonhuman, natural and unnatural.

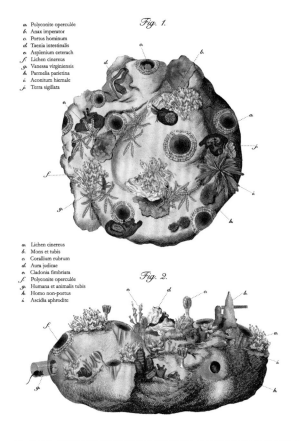

can in fact operate within architectural and landscape thinking to question as well as reinvent our relationship to objects and context, to engage in practices of 'dehabituation' that enable us to 'see things anew',[14] or simply to probe where we might be heading. Out of what kind of fog? Into what kind of New World?

The 'Ambiguous Territory' collection of works point to approaches that might avoid the false choices that continue to haunt both disciplines. These include: the naive conviction that architecture and landscape can and should be charged with solving the world's problems, as sustainability would have it; the fatalistic solipsism of a retreat into disciplinary autonomy, as a resurgent Postmodernism and other inward-looking formal practices would have it; or an abdication of architectural design altogether in favour of research conducted through the methods of disciplines external to architecture and landscape, such as geography or photography, as this issue of △ would seem to have it. By avoiding such traps, architects and landscape architects actualise their unique potential to engage the world on their own terms and through their own media. In doing so, the act of design is mobilised to make visible as well as tangible – in material, formal, spatial and even programmatic terms – in all of its alienating and potentially anxiety-inducing ways, the contemporary haunting of a planet estranged from itself and on the brink of profound transformations. △

Notes
1. Gursky's 'extraterrestrial view' is akin to the 'Archimedean point', Arendt's Sputnik flying above the earth; see Hannah Arendt, *The Human Condition*, University of Chicago Press (Chicago, IL), [1958] 1998, p 251.
2. Robert Enright, 'The Fine and Excruciating Construction of the World: An Interview with Ed Burtynsky', *Border Crossings*, 117, March 2011, pp 22–37.
3. Reyner Banham, *A Concrete Atlantis: US Industrial Building and European Modern Architecture*, MIT Press (Cambridge, MA), 1986, pp 194–215.
4. Reyner Banham, 'The Machine Aesthetic', *Architectural Review*, April 1955, p 226.
5. Perry Miller, *The Life of the Mind in America from the Revolution to the Civil War*, Harcourt, Brace & World (New York), 1965, p 305.
6. Banham, *A Concrete Atlantis*, op cit, p 197.
7. Reyner Banham, *Theory and Design in the First Machine Age*, MIT Press (Cambridge, MA), 1980, pp 320–30.
8. Walter Benjamin and Michael W Jennings, 'The Work of Art in the Age of Its Technological Reproducibility [First Version]', *Grey Room*, 39, Spring 2010, p 33.
9. Will Steffen *et al*, 'The Anthropocene: Conceptual and Historical Perspectives', *Philosophical Transactions of the Royal Society A*, 369 (1938), 2011, pp 842–67.
10. Siobhan Carroll, 'The Ecological Uncanny: On the *Southern Reach* Trilogy', *The Los Angeles Review of Books*, 5 October 2015: https://lareviewofbooks.org/article/the-ecological-uncanny-on-the-southern-reach-trilogy/#!.
11. Jennifer Peeples, 'Toxic Sublime: Imaging Contaminated Landscapes', *Environmental Communication: A Journal of Nature and Culture*, 5 (4), December 2011, p 375.
12. Barbara Creed and Jeanette Hoorn, 'Animals, Art, Abjection', in Rina Arya and Nicholas Chare (eds), *Abject Visions: Powers of Horror in Art and Visual Culture*, Manchester University Press (Manchester), 2016, p 91.
13. https://taubmancollege.umich.edu/research/ambiguous-territory.
14. David Wood, 'Can Only Art Save Us Now?', in Martin Drenthen and Jozef Keulartz (eds), *Environmental Aesthetics: Crossing Divides and Breaking Ground*, Fordham University Press (New York), 2014, p 128.

Ellie Abrons,
Inside Things,
2016

Inside Things comprises a series of abstract physical models, the material, formal and spatial characteristics of which promote general qualities of ambiguity, specifically in terms of misreading, openness to interpretation, and variable meaning. In this way, Abrons's work engages in a certain slippage between form and content, actively destabilising conventional distinctions between the formal and the formless, the architectural and the natural, the abstract and the figural.

CONTRIBUTORS

Merve Bedir graduated from the Middle East Technical University (METU) in Ankara (BArch) and the Delft University of Technology (TU Delft) in the Netherlands (PhD). Her work revolves around the politics of labour and design as non-disciplinary acts. She is the co-founder of Land and Civilization Compositions (Rotterdam/Pearl River Delta) and Aformal Academy, and a founding member of Kitchen (Gaziantep) and the Center for Spatial Justice (Istanbul). Her collaborative and multiscalar practice varies among research, exhibition and design projects. She has participated in the Oslo Triennale, Bucharest Art, Shenzhen and Venice Biennales, and her work has been reviewed in *Metropolis*, the *Avery Review* and the *Guardian*. She has written for *MIT Thresholds*, *Volume*, *Funambulist* and *Zivot*, among others.

Benjamin H Bratton is Professor of Visual Arts at the University of California, San Diego, and Program Director of the Strelka Institute of Media, Architecture and Design in Moscow. He is also a Professor of Digital Design at the European Graduate School and Visiting Faculty at the Southern California Institute of Architecture (SCI-Arc). He is the author of *The Stack: Software and Sovereignty* (MIT Press, 2015).

Ingrid Burrington is a writer, artist and the author of *Networks of New York: An Illustrated Field Guide to Urban Internet Infrastructure* (Melville House, 2016). Her work explores the technology of landscapes and the landscapes of technology. She has previously written for *The Atlantic*, *The Verge* and *The Nation*, and her work has previously been supported by the Eyebeam Art and Technology Center, Data & Society Research Institute and the Center for Land Use Interpretation.

Ian Cheng makes simulations that explore the nature of mutation and our capacity to relate to change. Drawing on principles of video-game design and cognitive science, his virtual ecosystems are populated with characters governed by competing models of artificial intelligence (AI). Each attempts to perpetuate its approach amid otherworldly environmental conditions. What emerges is an endless, unpredictable stream of artificial life.

Cathryn Dwyre is Adjunct Associate Professor at Pratt Institute's School of Architecture in New York. She received a Master of Landscape Architecture from the University of Pennsylvania in Philadelphia, and a BA in philosophy and geology from Colgate University. She is co-principal of the design practice pneumastudio with Chris Perry, with whom she was also a recipient of the MacDowell Colony Fellowship and co-editor of a special issue of *PAJ: A Journal of Performance and Art* (January 2015). She previously served as Managing Editor of ViaBooks and its volume *Dirt* (MIT Press). pneumastudio's work has been exhibited at the Onassis Cultural Centre in Athens, Greece, Storefront for Art and Architecture in New York, the Design Museum in Barcelona and New York University.

John Gerrard is best known for his sculpture and installation works, typically taking the form of digital simulations, made using real-time computer graphics. Born in Ireland, he received a BFA from the Ruskin School of Drawing and Fine Art, Oxford University in 1997 and completed his postgraduate studies at the School of the Art Institute of Chicago, Trinity College, Dublin, and at the Rijksakademie, Independent Residency Program, Amsterdam. Recent solo presentations include *Western Flag (Spindletop, Texas)*, commissioned by Channel 4 for Somerset House in London (2017), *Power.Play* at the Ullens Center for Contemporary Art in Beijing (2016), and *Solar Reserve (Tonopah, Nevada)*, Lincoln Center in association with the Public Art Fund, New York City (2014).

Alice Gorman is an internationally recognised leader in the field of space archaeology. She is a Senior Lecturer at Flinders University in Adelaide, Australia. Her research focuses on the archaeology and heritage of space exploration, including space junk, planetary landing sites, off-earth mining, rocket launchpads and antennas. She is a member of the American Institute of Aeronautics and Astronautics and the Space Industry Association of Australia. Her writing regularly appears in the *Best Australian Science Writing* anthology, and in 2017 she won the Bragg UNSW Press Prize for Science Writing.

Deborah Harrison is one of the original architects of the personality for Microsoft's digital assistant, Cortana. She crafted the core principles that define Cortana's approach to communication and helps teach deep neural networks to manifest distinct personalities. She currently leads a team that brings the same expertise in conversational user interface, inclusive design and machine learning to other intelligent products and features. She believes that while the field of AI is still in its adolescence, these in the industry stand in a brilliant position to shape not only technological innovation, but also the culture of communication between humans and machines.

Adam Harvey is an American artist and researcher, currently based in Berlin, exploring societal impacts of networked data analysis technologies with a focus on computer vision and counter-surveillance. He is a graduate of the Interactive Telecommunications Program at New York University (2010) and previously studied engineering and photojournalism at Pennsylvania State University.

Jason Hilgefort studied at the University of Cincinnati (BUP) and the University of British Columbia in Vancouver (MArch). He is the co-founder of Land and Civilization Compositions, Aformal Academy and the Institute for Autonomous Urbanism. He has worked with Peter Calthorpe, Rahul Mehrotra, Maxwan and ZUS. He led Maxwan's competition victories in Helsinki, Basel, Kiev, Brussels, Ostrava, Hanover and Lithuania before winning the Europan 11 challenge in Vienna. His academic experience includes TU Delft, the Università Iuav di Venezia (IUAV), Parsons School of Design in New York and HafenCity University in Hamburg. He was a sub-curator for the Shenzhen Biennale (2016) and co-director of its learning platform. He is also a contributor to *Site Magazine*.

Hyphen-Labs is an international team of women of colour working at the intersection of technology, art, science and the future. Through their global vision and unique perspectives they are driven to create meaningful and engaging ways to explore emotional, human-centred and speculative design. In the process they challenge conventions and stimulate conversations, placing collective needs and experiences at the centre of evolving narratives. Hyphen-Labs designs and builds robust transmedia experiences by combining new and old ideas, crafts and digital, physical mediums ranging in scale from small products and prototypes to large architectural pavilions and installations. Through their creative practice and artistic commissions, they blend architecture, speculative and interactive design, digital arts, fashion, creative writing and film through new media and emerging technologies.

Paul Inglis studied at London's Royal College of Art (RCA) before embarking on a film career spanning more than 20 years. He is currently working on *Star Wars Episode IX* for JJ Abrams. Other highlights to date include *Blade Runner 2049* and *Skyfall* (both with Dennis Gassner), *Mission Impossible*, *Jason Bourne* and *Children of Men*, along with supervising the pilot and first season of *Game of Thrones* for Gemma Jackson. He has won two Art Directors Guild awards as well as being nominated on four other occasions, and was the supervising art director for *The Young Victoria*, a film whose rich look garnered it an Academy Award nomination for Best Production Design. He lives and works in London.

Rem Koolhaas founded OMA in 1975 together with Elia and Zoe Zenghelis and Madelon Vriesendorp. He heads the work of both OMA and its research branch AMO, operating in areas beyond the realm of architecture. His built work includes the Garage Museum of Contemporary Art in Moscow (2015), Fondazione Prada, Milan (2015), the headquarters for China Central Television (CCTV) in Beijing (2012), Casa da Música in Porto (2005), Seattle Central Library (2004), and the Netherlands Embassy in Berlin (2003). He is a professor at Harvard University, and in 2014 was the director of the 14th Venice Architecture Biennale, entitled 'Fundamentals'.

Jesse LeCavalier is an associate professor of architecture at the New Jersey Institute of Technology in Newark, and the Daniel Rose Visiting Assistant Professor at the Yale School of Architecture in New Haven, Connecticut. He was the recipient of the 2015 New Faculty Teaching Award from the Association of the Collegiate Schools of Architecture (ACSA) and the 2010–11 Sanders Fellow at the University of Michigan. His project 'Shelf Life' was one of five finalists for the 2018 MoMA PS1 Young Architects Program. He is the author of *The Rule of Logistics: Walmart and the Architecture of Fulfillment* (University of Minnesota Press, 2016).

Xingzhe Liu is a multiple award-winning photographer and has covered stories domestically and internationally, including the Wenchuan earthquake, Libyan Revolution, Arab Spring and North Korea nuclear crisis. His current work focuses on China's urbanisation and Chinese youth. He is a contributing photographer to the @EyesOnChinaProject Instagram feed. Born in Chengdu, Sichuan province, he now lives and works in Shanghai.

Clare Lyster is an architect, writer and associate professor at the University of Illinois at Chicago. She is the author of *Learning From Logistics: How Networks Change Cities* (Birkhäuser, 2016), which explores the implications of logistics for architecture and urbanism. Her research on the topic has been exhibited at the Lisbon Architecture Triennale (2016), Seoul Biennale of Architecture and Urbanism (2017) and London Design Festival (2018).

Geoff Manaugh is the author of the *New York Times* bestselling book *A Burglar's Guide to the City* (FSG Originals, 2016), on the relationship between burglary and architecture. He is a former co-director of Studio-X NYC, an off-campus event space and urban futures think-tank at Columbia University, New York, and has taught at the Columbia Graduate School of Architecture, Planning and Preservation (GSAPP), the University of Southern California (USC) and SCI-Arc. He is also an active freelance journalist, regularly covering issues related to design, cities, crime, infrastructure and technology for the *New York Times Magazine*, *The Atlantic* and many other publications. His short story 'Ernest', published by *VICE*, is being adapted for film by Legendary Entertainment.

Tim Maughan is an author and journalist using both fiction and non-fiction to explore issues around cities, class, culture, technology and the future. His work regularly appears on the BBC, in the *New Scientist* and *Vice/Motherboard*. His debut novel *Infinite Detail* will be published by FSG in 2019. He also collaborates with artists and filmmakers, and has had work shown at the Victoria and Albert Museum, London, Columbia School of Architecture, Vienna Biennale and on Channel 4. He currently lives in Canada.

Simone C Niquille is a designer and researcher based in Amsterdam. Her practice Technoflesh investigates the representation of identity and the digitisation of biomass in the networked space of appearance. She holds a BFA in Graphic Design from Rhode Island School of Design and an MA in Visual Strategies from the Sandberg Instituut Amsterdam. She currently teaches design research at ArtEZ University of the Arts in Arnhem, the Netherlands. She is a 2016 Fellow of Het Nieuwe Instituut in Rotterdam, and recipient of a talent development grant from the Creative Industries Fund NL (2016–17). She was also a contributor to the Dutch Pavilion at the 2018 Venice Architecture Biennale.

Jenny Odell is an Oakland-based artist and writer whose work argues for the rewards of close observation, especially as a way of participating in one's physical environment. Her work has been exhibited internationally, and she has been an artist in residence at Recology SF (a waste-processing centre), the Internet Archive and the San Francisco Planning Department. She teaches digital/physical design at Stanford University in California.

Trevor Paglen is an artist whose work spans image-making, sculpture, investigative journalism, writing, engineering and numerous other disciplines. Among his chief concerns are learning how to see the historical moment we live in and developing the means to imagine alternative futures. His work has featured in solo exhibitions at the Vienna Secession, Eli & Edythe Broad Art Museum, Van Abbe Museum, Frankfurter Kunstverein and Protocinema Istanbul, in group exhibitions at the Metropolitan Museum of Art, San Francisco Museum of Modern Art and Tate Modern, among others, and in the *New York Times*, *The New Yorker*, *Vice Magazine* and *Art Forum*. He is the author of five books as well as many articles on subjects including experimental geography, state secrecy, military symbology, photography and visuality.

Chris Perry is Associate Professor and Associate Dean at the School of Architecture, Rensselaer Polytechnic Institute, in New York. He received a Master of Architecture from Columbia University and a BA in philosophy from Colgate University. He is co-principal of the design practice pneumastudio with Cathryn Dwyre, with whom he was a joint recipient of the MacDowell Colony Fellowship and co-editor of a special issue of *PAJ: A Journal of Performance and Art* (January 2015). He is a recipient of the Architectural League's Young Architects Award and co-guest-editor of ∆ *Collective Intelligence in Design* (September/October 2006).

Ben Roberts is a British photographer. He is based in Madrid, but shoots on assignment globally for international magazines and brands, photographing a broad range of subjects. His job takes him behind the scenes and into extraordinary situations: he has shot a rave on a cruise ship, gypsy musicians in Transylvania, the inside of an Amazon warehouse and refugees arriving into Europe.

David Salomon is an assistant professor of art history and coordinator of the Architectural Studies programme at Ithaca College in London. He is a co-author of *The Architecture of Patterns* (WW Norton, 2010). His research on a wide range of architectural topics – from symmetry to supermarkets – has been published in *Grey Room*, *Log*, *Harvard Design Magazine*, *Places*, the *Journal of Architecture*, *Journal of Landscape Architecture* and *Journal of Architectural Education*.

Kathy Velikov is a founding partner of rvtr, an associate professor at the Taubman College of Architecture and Urban Planning, University of Michigan, and President of ACADIA. Her work explores the agency of architecture and urban design within the context of dynamic ecological systems, infrastructures, materially and technologically mediated environments, and emerging social organisations. She is a recipient of the Architectural League's Young Architects Award and the Canadian Professional Prix de Rome in Architecture, and is co-author of the book *Infra Eco Logi Urbanism* (Park Books, 2015).

What is *Architectural Design*?

Founded in 1930, *Architectural Design* (⌀) is an influential and prestigious publication. It combines the currency and topicality of a newsstand journal with the rigour and production qualities of a book. With an almost unrivalled reputation worldwide, it is consistently at the forefront of cultural thought and design.

Each title of ⌀ is edited by an invited Guest-Editor, who is an international expert in the field. Renowned for being at the leading edge of design and new technologies, ⌀ also covers themes as diverse as architectural history, the environment, interior design, landscape architecture and urban design.

Provocative and pioneering, ⌀ inspires theoretical, creative and technological advances. It questions the outcome of technical innovations as well as the far-reaching social, cultural and environmental challenges that present themselves today.

For further information on ⌀, subscriptions and purchasing single issues see:

http://onlinelibrary.wiley.com/journal/10.1002/%28ISSN%291554-2769

Volume 88 No 1
ISBN 978 1119 379515

Volume 88 No 2
ISBN 978 1119 254416

Volume 88 No 3
ISBN 978 1119 332633

Volume 88 No 4
ISBN 978 1119 337843

Volume 88 No 5
ISBN 978 1119 328148

Volume 88 No 6
ISBN 978 1119 375951

How to Subscribe
With 6 issues a year, you can subscribe to ⌀ (either print, online or through the ⌀ App for iPad)

Institutional subscription
£310 / $580
print or online

Institutional subscription
£388 / $725
combined print and online

Personal-rate subscription
£136 / $215
print and iPad access

Student-rate subscription
£90 / $137
print only

⌀ App for iPad
6-issue subscription:
£44.99 / US$64.99
Individual issue:
£9.99 / US$13.99

To subscribe to print or online
E: cs-journals@wiley.com

Americas
E: cs-journals@wiley.com
T: +1 781 388 8598
or +1 800 835 6770
(toll free in the USA & Canada)

Europe, Middle East and Africa
E: cs-journals@wiley.com
T: +44 (0) 1865 778315

Asia Pacific
E: cs-journals@wiley.com
T: +65 6511 8000

Japan (for Japanese-speaking support)
E: cs-japan@wiley.com
T: +65 6511 8010
or 005 316 50 480
(toll-free)

Visit our Online Customer Help available in 7 languages at www.wileycustomerhelp.com/ask